"Tammy is an exub͟ ... ping true story of divorce, betrayal, devastation and recovery inspires healing and hope in women who are dealing with the despair of a relationship breakup."

—Nancy Nichols, Author of *Secrets of the Ultimate Husband Hunter: How to Attract Men, Enjoy Dating and Recognize the Love of Your Life*

"If you are serious about shifting into a new reality and leaving behind your past, then this book is for you. If you are not serious, then do yourself a favor and save your money. This inspiring story of perseverance over pressure, and triumph over tragedy will have breaking the levees of limitation off your life once and for all. This book is a brilliant! WOW ... go Tammy."

—Simon T. Bailey, Author of *Release Your Brilliance*

"*When the Levee Breaks* is brilliant, yes, and it is also warm and moving removing all screens of pretense about surviving the challenges of life. If you put together the best of Anthony Robbins, Marshall Sylver, and Wayne Dyer, what you would have would be almost as good as Tammy King."

—Grace Major, Real Estate Investor

"I met Tammy when chance made me her supervisor. We worked in an office with eight other women. One office, ten women, can you imagine the drama? Shortly after I began work there, one of our coworkers made a statement to Tammy that I could see hurt her in some way. But I already knew her, who she was and what she would become. She just didn't know it yet. I remember what I said to her, and that has not changed. "Tammy, do not worry about some small hurtful comment today, for when these women look back in life, they will not say about you, that you were cute or sweet or smart; they will say, she changed my life." And so, she has become a life changer."

—Kathy Haynes, Owner Haynes & Howell General Contractors, Inc.

"Tammy and I have been friends for over 25 years. She has always had the best attitude and the bubbliest personality, no matter what she is going through or what is going on around her. We all go through struggles in our daily life, but to be able to keep the faith and attitude that she has at all times is amazing to me. I promise, when you start to read one of her books, you will not be able to put it down."

—Krissy Moss Lavelle, Lifelong Friend

"I have known Tammy King for 10 years and as a business owner, mother, and survivor of change myself, have been truly inspired by her faith, perseverance, and tenacity in dealing with all of the changes she has been through. Tammy is a warrior, and even in her weak times she knew that she and her children would be fine and that somehow, with God's grace,

she would find a way to the light at the end of the tunnel. Her inspiring story has helped numerous women going through life changes and has inspired us to look to our Heavenly Father and the strength that He has placed inside of each of us to weather the floods when the levee breaks."
—Kelly Dobbins, Owner, Mid-South Drug Testing

"*When the Levee Breaks*" is a heart-warming rendition of a life ripped apart by loss that becomes an inspirational tale of hope, faith, healing and personal growth. It is a story of the person, I believe, we all strive to become."
—Abbey Rihtarshick, University of Phoenix Alumni

"I love the sharing of your story! I share your pain, I see your heart, and I feel your purpose on each page! Honored to have been given this glimpse into your struggles, I celebrate the blessing your book will be to those who have found themselves in the midst of loss, with all the pain and panic that are often part of that package. I love the personal restoration and renewal found between these pages! Most of all I love the title *When the Levee Breaks* and the wonderful lesson of rescue! That analogy is brilliant!"
—Marilyn Cullum, Grace for the Journey Ministries
Licensed Professional Counselor and
Certified Life Purpose Coach

when
the levee
breaks

Mark,
You Rock!

Harry

tammy king

when the levee breaks

holding on when life lets go

TATE PUBLISHING & Enterprises

Published by Tate Publishing & Enterprises, LLC
127 E. Trade Center Terrace | Mustang, Oklahoma 73064 USA
1.888.361.9473 | www.tatepublishing.com

Tate Publishing is committed to excellence in the publishing industry. The company reflects the philosophy established by the founders, based on Psalm 68:11,
"The Lord gave the word and great was the company of those who published it."

Book design copyright © 2010 by Tate Publishing, LLC. All rights reserved.
Cover design by Amber Gulilat
Interior design by Stefanie Rooney

Published in the United States of America

ISBN: 978-1-61663-674-6
1. Religion, Christian Life, Inspirational
2. Religion, Christian Life, Personal Growth
10.06.24

Dedication

This book is dedicated to

my mom, *Carolyn King*.

I love you!

Acknowledgments

With heartfelt thanks:

First, to my Savior and friend, Jesus, I am amazed by Your love for me. Without You, I would have never survived. You are the Lord of my life, and I give You praise. May the message You have placed within me, the words You have allowed me to express, and the life that You have given me bring You glory.

To my mom, Carolyn King, I have learned about this thing called life from you. You have been an incredible example of strength, wisdom, dedication, and love my entire life. It is with a grateful heart that I can say, without a doubt, you are the best mom any daughter could ever have.

To my children, Ashley, Kasey, Kelly, and Travis—you are the reason I never gave up. I am so blessed to be your mom. I am so proud of each one of you, and you will always be my babies no matter how "grown" you get! May God bless you and keep you. Live your life for Him, and never forget how much you are loved.

To my brother, Brad King, his wife, Erin, and my nephew, Connor—you are the definition of what family is all about. Together, we have seen our share of good times and bad, and through it all we have been there for each other. I love you.

To Melanie Carnahan, Deb Dunlap, Loretta McNary, and Amanda Phelps—what a ride it's been! We've experienced a little bit of everything since we all met just a couple of years ago. You have become like sisters to me. Thank you for being there to hold me up when I was too tired to tread the water anymore. You are the most fabulous women on the planet and everything—everything—we've seen will come to pass!

To Nancy Lee (www.ronleehomes.com) and the entire NAWIC Chapter number 339 from New Orleans, LA—little did you know that you would be a pivotal piece of God's plan for my life! (You probably didn't know that you'd end up in an upcoming book of mine, either.) All of you are so precious to me. Each of you is a gift that God placed in my life at just the right moment. Nancy, the trip that you arranged for me to come and speak in October 2008 saved my dreams from being swept away when the levee broke around me. I will always, always be in your debt. Ladies, I cannot wait to see you again! I'm looking forward to being at the Superdome—Wy and I will stop by on our way there to pick you up!

To my extended family and to the friends who have been there throughout my life—I consider you all to be incredible blessings from God. Thank you for your prayers. Thank you for your encouragement. You are priceless treasures to me. Many of you prayed for me when I could barely pray for myself. May the love you have shown toward me be returned to you a hundred fold!

Lastly, to Richard Tate, Trinity Tate, Dave Dolphin, Meghan Barnes, and the entire staff at Tate Publishing—thank you for believing in a dreamer like me! I know that few get the opportunity that you have so graciously given me, and it is my prayer that together, we continue to provide material that will encourage, inspire, and uplift the spirit man within each of us. I am humbled and honored to be a part of the Tate Publishing family.

Table of Contents

Foreword

Just like the break of a physical levee, things are destroyed and changed; so are we when we go through personal (spiritual) storms—we are forever changed. Yet there is hope, for Psalm 91:11–12 and 14–15, makes this promise, "For He will command His angels concerning you to guard you in all of your ways; they will lift you up in their hands, so that you will not strike your foot against a stone. 'Because He loves me,' says the Lord, 'I will rescue him; I will protect him, for he acknowledges My name. He will call upon Me and I will answer him; I will be with him in trouble. I will deliver him and honor him.'"

When the Levee Breaks is an anchor for those of

us who experience life in 3-D. I am talking about life that "happens" in wave after wave after wave. I lived through and survived many storms in 3-D, as I am sure so have many of you. Storm number one hits and turns your world upside down; it could be the loss of a job, a repossessed car, or a sick child. A few months or weeks later, when you have barely gotten over the last episode of your life's challenge and you have just exhaled, you get knocked back off your feet by storm number two: one of your parents become seriously ill or there is an unfaithful spouse. You finally see the sun shining in the distance again. You have planted your feet, things are back on track, and here comes another wave; not quite a storm, but there is a huge setback nonetheless. After this hit you may have started bargaining with God like I did. "Okay, Lord, we got all of this settled. I am good for at least a few years, right?"

A few months later here comes another wave, this one is bigger than the last two. Now because the hit was totally by surprise and unexpected, you begin to question and doubt that God really cares. Especially since you and God, according to your memory, had agreed that it was time for some good 'ole soothing, peaceful, calming sunshine. You even reminded God about how strong you were in the previous storms. You shared with him how you survived and did not move "too far" away from Him. You rationalized that surely God understands that you are tired and weary. He must know that you cannot take much more of this before you break. And you did break, at least temporarily. And miraculously your questions are answered, your doubts disappear, and peace abides on your shore. Once more, you see the sunshine in the midst of the clouds. Each day, you grow stronger; you adjust to your "new normal" and are set on cruise control. Life is good, so you decide to give God another chance. You pray every day, attend church most Sundays, pay your tithes when you can, and help out your neighbors. You got it all figured out; you are living in peace in spite of all you have been through. You are singing a new song of praise and worship. You tell everyone, "God is good. Praise the Lord, everybody." Then one day the phone rings, and here comes another unpredicted storm of horrendous magnitude and range. "Oh no, this can't be happening, Lord. This is way too much for me. What do you do now that the entire levee has broken?"

Tammy King has written about and re-lived her most tumultuous storms in *When the Levee Breaks* just to minister to us. Tammy reveals that she knew, spiritually, that through all the hurt and pain, it was not going to "take her out" because there is purpose in every storm. She knew as a young girl that God had a master plan for her life to help others to know that we have divine purpose in our lives. *When the Levee Breaks* walks us through step by step, how to survive intact the raging storms of life and still be able to give God glory, honor, and praise. Tammy inspires us to hold on tight, and hang on no matter what to God. We learn to believe what the Word says, instead of what the storms say. Jesus spoke to the storm and said, "Peace be still." We need to tell our storms, "Peace be still," tell the mountains to crumble and get out of our way, and tell the devil he is defeated. I encourage you, along with Tammy, when the levee breaks, rest assured that the levee cannot "take you out" as long as you hold on and hang on to God's unchanging hand. He is reaching out to you; take His hand. *When the Levee Breaks* is proof that God cares and is always with us, and it reminds us that the Son is always shining, even when the levee breaks.

Loretta McNary, TV Talk Show Host
The Loretta McNary Show
www.lorettamcnary.com

Part One

Answer me quickly, O Lord, my spirit fails. Do not hide your face from me or I will be like those who go down to the pit. Let the morning bring me word of your unfailing love, for I have put my trust in you. Show me the way I should go, for to you I lift up my soul. Teach me to do your will, for you are my God, may your good Spirit lead me on level ground.

Psalm 143:7–8, 10

Introduction

There are times that we go through in life that mark significant places for us. Some of those times are filled with great joy, and some are filled with loss and pain. The following chapters were written during a very trying season. My family's financial stability was removed, my father suffered three major strokes, and my teenagers began testing the water in the world around them. But of all the things that I faced, my faith and my spirit remained bent on praise and steadfastness and assurance that everything was going to be fine, and in those particular situations, everything was. Those were difficult but somehow easy at the same time. It wasn't until

I encountered a devastating blow within my church that the storm became too much. My life went from a constant pounding of rain to an all-out hurricane. Little did I know as the final onslaught of wind and rain began to fall in July that by the end of October of that same year, I would be caught up in the ravenous storm, unable to catch my breath …

Change Is Coming

There is a time for everything, and a season for
every activity under heaven.

Ecclesiastes 3:1

A decision has to be made. Not a regular
"what's for dinner?" kind of decision, but a
life-changing, whole-lot-of-people-involved, don't-
want-to mess-this-up kind of decision. Some say that
I am making a big deal out of nothing, but there's a
rumbling in my spirit that convinces me that this one
is huge.

For several years now I have been following hard
after Christ. I've followed Him up hills, around
mountains, and through a few valleys, and although
it has not always been easy, it has always been reward-

ing. There is something about walking with Jesus that is extremely satisfying, no matter where He has led you or what He has led you through. He leads, guides, and directs our paths, and I believe that with all my heart. There is just one small problem; He just turned a corner in my life, and I am not sure which way He went. I know that He hasn't gone far because He says that He will never leave me nor forsake me, but I promise you, for the life of me, I do not know which way He just turned. The path that we were traveling on suddenly dead-ended, and that can only mean one thing: life as I know it is about to change, and that has me a little concerned.

Changes take place for everyone; I am very aware of that. I also know that most people handle them really well. The trouble is, I am not one of those people. I am highly against change. Changes of any kind tend to bring about major emotional turmoil for me. It is not that I do not like new things; I just don't like the process of letting go of the old thing to get there. The transition from the old to the new has many times broken my heart. This time will surely be no different. Change is coming.

Change can take place over a period of time, or it can happen suddenly. Change always means that something, whether big or small, permanent or temporary, will take place. Three of the most exciting changes for me happened when I changed from being a single woman to a married one; when I changed from not having children to becoming a mother to four; and my favorite change of all was when I changed from someone lost and bound for hell to someone found and destined for heaven. These were incredible times of joyful changes in my life, but sadly for me they are not the ones that tend to be the first things I think about when I know that change is near. No, the ones that replay first are the ones that have shattered my heart.

I remember when as a small child my innocence changed to shame. I remember as a teenager when a pregnancy changed to a miscarriage, and as I write these words, the pain is still fresh from when a dream of mine changed into a nightmare just a year ago. These are the things that have happened that cause my insides to tremble at the very thought of change, and this is why the decision that needs to be made very soon has me begging God to show me which way I should go.

Come Closer

Come near to God and He will come near to you.
James 4:8

How did I get to this place? How does life go from comfortable to crazy in a matter of minutes? How can everything be so right and yet so temporary? The answers to these questions may not be answered on this side of heaven. This life we lead here on earth is full of surprises, questions, tears, and laughter.

Being so far from home it's no wonder things feel out of place. We live in earthly vessels led by our spiritual man, and while we're trying to work things out here, our spirit man is focused on the things above. He helps us walk the path God has set before us so that we reach our final destination—so that we reach our home in heaven. What makes this difficult at times is that God's plan for our lives often collides with our own plans. We pray for God's will and His direction but struggle to cooperate when it interferes with what we want. It's at these moments in our lives things can begin to go horribly wrong. We press on going our own way until we are hit head-on with the consequences of our actions. And man, what a mess that creates! We find ourselves at the scene of an accident where our will and God's will have collided. Some accidents only cause superficial damage with a small scratch here or there, but sometimes accidents are fatal. Twisted metal, critical injuries, and complete devastation; whatever the outcome, accidents are rarely pleasant, and in our Christian walk they are many times unavoidable.

It is my prayer that the lessons I learned while trying to find my way in a place I never dreamed I would be will help you, strengthen you, and encourage you in your own journey and draw you closer to Jesus Christ. He beckons us to come closer. That's what I want—a closer walk with Jesus. I want a relationship with my Savior that sustains me through good times and bad and helps me find my way closer to Him day by day. A closer walk awaits you. A deeper fulfillment is yours. Will you come closer?

Houston?

Trust in the Lord with all your heart, and lean not on your own understanding; in all your ways acknowledge Him, and He will make your paths straight.

Proverbs 3:5–6

When was the last time you took a good look at where you were in life? Maybe it was January 1, or perhaps it was your birthday. Maybe you've been so busy living life that you can't remember the last time you stopped long enough to even see where you are. For me it took a split in the road. This decision that needs to be made has given me no choice but to stop and take a good look at where I am and where I want to be. Am I where God wants me to be, and is His plan for my life the one I am pursuing?

The choices surrounding me right now are overwhelming. Have you ever been there? Trying to make a clear decision in the middle of your circumstances is impossible sometimes. Apparently God knew that I was going to need some time to think this one through, so in His perfect timing, He arranged a way for me to get away for some much-needed rest and relaxation. My girlfriends had been planning a trip to Houston, Texas, for about six months to attend a First Place conference. They had asked me to join them several times, but I had refused to go because of my job. Things were busy. I was needed. Even if I could get away from work, I still had a husband and four kids that surely wouldn't be okay if I left for a week. So, I never asked God. I never thought that I should've just run the trip by Him. I just told my girlfriends I'd take a rain check. Little did I know that this trip was already predestined by the God who loves me, and He would make sure that I did not miss it.

The "Ripping"

We are hard pressed on every side, but not crushed;
perplexed, but not in despair; persecuted, but not
abandoned; struck down, but not destroyed.

2 Corinthians 4:8–9

"We are very disappointed in you."
That is the statement that sent me
over the edge and on my way to Houston. Those were
the words that sent my perfectly planned-out future
into a mess. Now this may not seem like a big deal
to most, but let me explain. I had started working
for my church in December of the previous year. My
husband had a great job, and we were in a position
where I could accept a job to work for my church

in exchange for our children's tuition at our church's private school. Five months later our family took a devastating blow when after twelve years, my husband's company decided they could manage without him. We were no longer in a position where I could afford to trade tuition for a salary, but I had agreed to work for that, and I loved my job, so I asked God to work things out. I knew that He had placed me there, and I also knew that I did not want to leave.

I thought my prayers had been answered when the new bookkeeper for the school left. I was given his part-time job, which paid $375.00 a week. It may not be a lot to most people, but to me it meant food and clothing for my family. He left the third week in May. I took over his responsibility but was not given his pay. My husband was asking for my help. We really needed the money, and I just knew that this was my answer, but I didn't want to ask for it. I wanted the board members to say something—they never did.

On a Friday afternoon in July, I asked my pastor about the money. Let's just say that it didn't go quite like I had expected. Still he said he would talk to the board. We had a regular meeting scheduled for Monday, and as the meeting came to a close, I asked Pastor if I could ask the men about the money. He asked me to leave and told me that he would take care of it. I was so excited.

I remember getting into my car with two of my daughters. I told them that I had asked for the money, and together we thanked God for His provision. As I drove home, I was so happy because I knew I was going to get to help my family, and as I was thanking God for what was being done in the board room, I heard this still, small voice in my spirit, "If it's nothing, you're done." For a moment, I thought, *Done ... well, there's no way I'm done, and there's no way the answer could be nothing.* I didn't know what they would do, but I did know that they would do something.

Tuesday morning I arrived at work, and shortly after that my pastor came in, and then came a board member. I was called in the office and asked to close the door and sit down. What followed ripped my heart out. Even my worst enemy had never spoken to me the way that I was spoken to that morning. I was told I was dishonorable, that I was a disappointment, and that the board was ashamed of me. I had no right to ask for money and was told that I would get nothing. When he finished, I explained to him that my children's tuition covered the secretary job I held, not the bookkeeper's job. He then told me that the bookkeeper had volunteered and that he wasn't paid. My pastor just sat there knowing that we had paid him and that was the reason I had asked for the money in the first place.

They told me that my husband just needed to go back to work, but he and I had decided that he should take some time off. This didn't go over well with my pastor because of the money my husband's job provided for the church. It wasn't about what was best for my family. It was about what was best for them. I told my pastor that I would do whatever it took to allow my husband to stay at home for a while, just like his wife had done for him. He leaned across the desk and said, "Tammy, she was a nurse. What in the world are you going to do?" I was shocked. What? What did he just say to me? In that moment, as my flesh began to react, I felt the peace of God settle me, and in my spirit, in that still small voice, I heard, "Sshhh, it's okay. I've got this." And with that, without me saying another word, the meeting was over.

The tears fell faster than I could catch them, and I could hardly catch my breath as we all stood to leave. For someone who's known for talking too much, I'm certain that my silence was noticed. I felt so humiliated and mistreated. Nothing could have ever prepared me for what had just happened, and I needed to go home. I finished the reports I was working on and left for the day, unsure of whether things would ever be the same. All the way home, I kept hearing the words that I'd heard the night before, "If it's nothing, you're done." How was nothing an option? I had gone over and above what was expected of me. I was doing the job of two previous employees that had made triple what my kids' tuition totaled. I had done this because I wanted to be a blessing to my church. I wanted to help them, and I felt like I had. Now I needed their help, but they had refused it. What would my husband say? What about my girls? What should I do? I was completely overwhelmed, and I knew I needed to get away.

My girlfriends were leaving for Texas the following Wednesday. With my husband's blessing, I called and told them I'd be there. I wasn't as needed at work as I had previously thought. That Monday I asked my pastor if I could have a few days off so I could go to Houston. He asked me why I was going, and I simply replied, "I don't know." It sounded so crazy, but it was the truth. All I knew was that I needed some time to get a hold of myself and to get alone with God—not to mention I desperately needed some girlfriend time. What followed was one of the most incredible weeks of my life.

On a Mission

You will seek Me and find Me when you seek Me
with all your heart.

Jeremiah 29:13

I showed up that Wednesday morning at seven am. Suitcases packed, Bible in hand, and a T-shirt that said "On a Mission." Uncertain of why I was there but sure that I was supposed to be, I was ready to go to Texas. We gathered around in a circle as my husband prayed for us. I kissed him good-bye, hugged my kids, and crawled into the back seat of a Suburban with my friends.

As we backed down the driveway, a final inspection was done. "Does everybody have all their luggage, their Bible, their books? Did you bring a swim-suit? Do we have water and snacks?" And last but not least, "Who's got the map?" It's right here—we've got it—we're ready.

I took a deep breath, looked out the window, and thanked God for what He was about to do in my life—even though I had no clue what that would be. I was on a mission to seek Him and to follow Him to Texas. There was an anticipation and an expectation that I'd never felt before. God had gone to great lengths to get me in this vehicle, and I could hardly wait. So I asked Him to show me everything because I didn't want to miss anything.

These are a few things that I learned on our trip to and from Houston:

1. A map is very helpful when you are traveling.

2. Everybody needs a break.

3. The food at some places can make you very ill.

4. You can't stay in Neverland forever.

5. Road construction can cause major delays.

6. Time can ease your pain.

7. Sometimes healing means laughing until you wet your pants.

8. Sometimes the road ahead is not clearly marked.

9. The 610 loop in Houston can keep you busy for hours.

10. God is faithful, and He is a very present help in time of need.

These lessons that I learned will stay with me forever. They helped me to understand a little better just what this life is really all about. I came home stronger, happier, and a little surer of who I was and who God was preparing me to be. I was prepared to make a decision, even if it wasn't the one I would have chosen.

I'd like to highlight a few things from this trip with you as we continue on our journey together. They helped me, and I pray that they will help you too.

Where's the Map?

I know, O Lord, that a man's life is not his own; it
is not for man to direct his steps.

Jeremiah 10:23

A map is very helpful when you are traveling.
One of the most important things we car-
ried with us to Houston was the map. We could see
where we were starting from and where we wanted
to end up. The map also helped us to plan our route
across three states. There were several ways we could
have gone that would have taken us to the same
place. We could have gone north and then headed
south. We could have gone south and then went
west. Or we could have gone west and then south.

Any of these ways would have ultimately taken us to Houston; the choice was up to us. Three routes—one destination. Sometimes this same thing can happen to us. As Christians, we have a destination for our lives. God has created each of us with a unique destiny and an ultimate purpose while we are here on this earth.

As I thought about this, I realized that a map of my life would be very useful. Just locating myself on my map would be nice—much less trying to figure out where I was headed—and even if that was possible, I'd still have to choose the route I would take to get there. Whew! It sounds like a lot of work, but at this point I'm willing to try just about anything because if I'm not real sure where I am, how can I know where I am headed? And if I don't know where I am headed, how can I determine what direction I should be going with my life? I had to start by asking myself a few questions and stopping to think about a few things.

Am I satisfied with my life? In my life, how important is my relationship with Christ? Am I regularly praying and reading God's Word? What am I most pleased with in my life? What would I change if I could? What do I like about me? What would I like to change? When am I the happiest? Who am I? Where am I? Oh, so many things!

Between this trip that we were taking and the decision that I had to make, I was forced to find myself on my map. I asked myself these questions, and I sought God through prayer and His Word. It's okay to admit we're not sure where we are or where we want to be, but it's not okay to know it and then not do anything about it.

Take some time and think about what some of those answers would be for you. It will help you to locate where you are today in your life. They will also be helpful in locating where you are headed. Take a few minutes for you. Spend some time in prayer. Thank God for the good things, and ask Him to help you with any areas that aren't so good.

Once you begin to take a serious look at your life and find out where you are, you can begin to see where you are headed and which way you are going to take to get there. You've got to have a plan, and not just any plan; you need God's plan. Then you have to take responsibility for your next move. No one else is responsible to get you to the destination He has planned for you. There's no riding shotgun in real life. Grab your map, locate your starting point, seek God for your ending point, and ask Him to help you choose the best way to get there. Your map will become a valuable tool for you. Over time it will help you to stay focused and remain on course. God has prepared for you great and mighty things. Live each day with passion and purpose, knowing where you are and where you are headed!

Neverland, Never Again

Though He brings grief, He will show compassion, so great is His unfailing love.

Lamentations 3:32

"You can't stay in Neverland forever." Those were words of wisdom from a dear friend. Her statement made me realize that I do like the fairytale world and that it was time for me to face the fact that everybody, including me, has to see things from the real-world perspective. There is nothing make-believe about the lives we live, but there was a part of me that liked the idea of a place where little girls are protected and unborn babies don't die. Where your past can be irrelevant and every day ends with happily ever after.

Her words forced me to ask myself why the fairytale life was so appealing to me, and my answers helped to open my eyes to underlying fear, anger, and sadness. If life was not a fairytale, then the world I had convinced myself existed really didn't, and if that place did not exist, then could everything that I was afraid of really be true? The answer was yes.

We do live in a world where little girls (and boys) are hurt. It happens every day, and no one is safe from the evil that lurks around us. My make-believe world let me cover the pain I had felt from abuse that happened when I was a little girl. The problem was the pain did not need to be covered up but healed. This is also true of the child I lost at the age of eighteen. My baby was what I thought would make all the bad things that had happened good.

I loved being pregnant. I felt alive. Believe it or not, this baby would be the very thing that would begin the process of God delivering me from my religious way of life and bringing me into a true, genuine relationship with Him, although the entire process would get far worse before it got better. I remember for the first time ever just talking to God. I knew he had blessed me with this beautiful life inside of me, and I was so thankful. My religious mindset even convinced me that God was pleased with me even though I had conceived this baby outside of marriage. This baby was proof that He loved me and was pleased with me, right? I remember times when I would place my hand on my stomach and just cry because I was so filled with joy, and that's why, when I miscarried my baby after fourteen weeks for no apparent reason, I turned my back on God and ran as fast as I could.

In Neverland, I would not have had my baby taken away. In Neverland, I would have never been mistreated and abused. In Neverland, the Hero would have protected me and kept this bad stuff from happening—so Neverland was where I wanted to be.

These are things that I have had to face as I have turned back to the God who had always loved me. He was my Hero, even when I convinced myself He didn't care. Ladies, I don't know what you have been through, but I do know that God does care, and if we will allow Him the opportunity to show us—He will. It took years before I understood that He, too, was upset when I was abused, and that He also grieved with me when I lost my baby. He is our King of Kings and Lord of Lords. He is our Alpha and Omega, and He is our Prince of Peace. He is the Hero that will never leave us nor forsake us, and He is the Hero that will fight for us and protect us— even from ourselves.

Until my friend spoke those words, I had not realized that I had carved out a place in my life called Neverland. I realized that it was not as pleasant as I had made it out to be. It was a place of denial and pain and a place I could stay where I refused to grow up and face life like an adult. Oh, my enemy likes for me to dwell there, and he does not want me to go—but my Hero is calling me to come out of there. It's time to move on. It is time to face reality and get on with my future. It is time to realize what is truth and to act on it.

Step out and take a walk with your Hero. Let God lead you to a place, a real place, of forgiveness, healing, and restoration. We can't pretend that life does not hurt at times, and we cannot decide to take up residence in a fairytale place. No, ladies, we can't stay in Neverland forever.

Go with me, go with God, and let's leave Neverland behind.

Rx: Laughter

Those who sow in tears will reap with songs of joy.

Psalm 125:5

Sometimes healing means laughing until you wet your pants.

In the first part of the book, I mentioned that I had watched a dream of mine turn into a nightmare. Would it surprise you to know that I shared this dream with my two best friends? What would you say if I told you that the same week we went to Houston was the exact same week everything had fallen apart the year before?

My friends taking me to Houston were the same

friends I had started a ministry outreach program with a couple of years previous. We basically had a building in the middle of town that we used twice a month. We did a Ladies' Night Out event on the first Friday of every month and a Saturday Night Jam for youth the second Saturday. From time to time there would also be Bible studies, exercise classes, and an occasional business meeting or birthday party. Everything was going well until the summer of our first year. For reasons I may never know, God allowed circumstances concerning me to escalate to the point where I found myself in a place where I had no choice but to pack up and leave, and leaving there was one of the hardest things I had ever had to do.

Have you ever been at a place that you loved? A place where you thought everything was going great, only to find out that you had somehow totally missed it: a place where you were completely oblivious to the trouble it was actually causing? Well I have, and I was smack in the middle of it right then.

I thought I had reached the place where I would minister forever, but forever was about to end abruptly, at least for now. Within two days I went from planning to packing. Everything changed. My girlfriends and I spent one final evening in the building praying and crying together. We weren't sure at the time why things were happening the way they were, but we were sure that God did, and we were sure that He would help us get through it.

By the end of that week, the dream and my heart had been shattered. It took four trucks, two trailers, and two trips to clear out all the stuff. I watched the chairs, the speakers, the books—all of it—being brought out and then placed in storage. As we came back for the last load, I knew I was supposed to let it go, but how? How do you let go of something that means so much? What had I done that deserved this? What did this mean? So many questions were flooding my head. It was one of the most crushing things I had ever felt in all of my days. I nearly drowned in my tears. I actually think I felt my heart cracking. It was horrible. I remember like it was yesterday the way I felt as I walked to the bathroom inside the building. I remember sliding down the wall, placing my head in my hands and crying uncontrollably. So much had been done there. The kids, the ladies … my son had even publicly accepted Christ there. How was I supposed to just walk away? Why was God allowing this to happen? What had gone so terribly wrong?

"Lord, where are You?" my heart cried out. "Do you not know that I need You right now?" At that moment, when I cried out to Him, I knew He was there. That peace that passes all understanding is so real. It was that peace that allowed me to wipe my eyes, stand to my feet, and finish what had to be done. I splashed cold water on my face, looked in the mirror, and I felt the Lord tell me to breathe. I turned around and walked out the bathroom door, gathered the last few things, and then headed for the back door.

As I turned around to take one last look, I saw a mess. Everything was a mess—including me. This wound would take a long time to heal, and I didn't even know how to start. I just wanted to go home and go to bed. Maybe I would feel better tomorrow. At least tomorrow would be Sunday and I could go to church—surely there I would feel better…

One would think that church would be a place where you could go and hold it all together. Tens of thousands do it every Sunday, but I'm not one of them. For someone known for her cheerfulness, it doesn't take long for someone to realize I ain't doin' so well. I cried from the first beat of the drum until the closing prayer. I'm not talking a few tears wiped away by a touch of a Kleenex; I'm talking all the makeup gone, towels ringing wet, moaning—I was completely out of control. Just when I thought I had it together, our beautiful music minister's wife steps up to sing, and she begins singing, "Breathe." It is one of the most powerful songs I have ever heard, and I felt God wrap His arms around me and again, I heard him speak to my heart, "Breathe."

Ladies, He is so in love with you, and no matter what has broken your heart, you have got to let Him near you. You've got to remain so close to Him that you can hear His heartbeat—even when you know that He could have prevented your broken heart in the first place. You trust Him because He is trustworthy. You don't have to understand any of it—you just have to know that He does. His ways are not our ways, and if we fail to trust Him through times of deep sorrow, we are headed for times that are much worse.

I wish I could say that after that morning I was back to my old self—happy and carefree—loving life and everything about it. No, I was still broken and hurt and sad and even a little angry. I had cried so hard at church that my pastor called me early that Monday morning. The churchy response would have been to tell him that I was fine, no big deal; I was just having a bad day, but that is not what happened. Somewhere between trying to explain what had happened and crying again, he managed to say a few words that made me feel a little better, even though my heart was broken. It was one of the hardest weeks I have ever endured, and it's one that causes me to tremble even now.

I didn't see my girlfriends as much over the next year. I knew they were praying for me and that they were waiting for me. I just wanted to be alone. Don't we do that? We separate ourselves from others, thinking it will help. I'm just thankful that they never gave up on me or the dream—even when I had. They were the ones who held me up when I didn't even realize I had let go, and they were the ones who asked me to go with them to Houston. It was this trip where healing finally took place for me in a way I least expected it—it came through laughter.

I had shed many tears over the past year, and now exactly one year later, I was about to cry for a different reason—I cried because I was happy. After all the yuck of the past year, I was surprised at just how much I had needed this trip and my girlfriends. We honestly laughed constantly. Everything was funny. We had the time of our lives. We spent one evening laughing so hard that one of us was always in the bathroom. It is probably more of the "you had to be there" kind of humor, so I won't go into a lot of details, but just know it was a time of hilarious, gut-wrenching laughter. We all should have had six-pack abs after Houston just from laughing. I don't know the number of times one of us yelled, "Shut up, I'm going to pee in my pants." In the car, in the hotel room, even at the First Place conference we were laughing, and along with the laughter came healing and restoration. I had survived. We had survived. I think that makes our enemy a little nervous, and you know what? I'm okay with that. The plan he had made backfired, and now we were stronger than ever! Thank You, Lord!

I have found that in the midst of all our pain, God has a plan and a purpose. And for every tear that falls, there will be some laughter. Only God knows why our hearts have to break and why the tears must fall, and only He knows what we need to heal. I have experienced more than one broken heart, and I have cried many tears. Has laughter always been what God has chosen to heal me? No, for the most part, it has simply required time. Time to pray. Time to read and meditate on God's Word. Time is a great healer, and so is laughter. Honestly, I'd choose the laughter over time any day because I'm allergic to pain. My body, my mind, and my spirit react strangely to pain and sadness. I'd much rather laugh than cry, but you know what? God has used those tears that have fallen and those painful cracks in my heart to minister to others. Only a God with complete control and infinite wisdom can do that. Jehovah, the Lord God Almighty, is the only One who can take something bad and turn it into good. He's the only One who can take the tears of sadness and turn them into tears of joy!

Missed Exits

"I will guide you in the way of wisdom and lead you along straight paths," says the Lord.

Proverbs 4:11

Sometimes the road ahead is not clearly marked. Okay. This is another real life lesson I learned in Houston. Have you ever been in unfamiliar territory and really needed some help? Have you ever found yourself traveling along, and after several hours (or days) you start thinking that you may have missed your turn? Yes? Great, me too!

Not that getting to Houston and finding our hotel and the church wasn't hard enough; I decided that I wanted to go to visit Beth Moore's office. Now you would think that every Christian woman who made it to Houston would have two goals. They would want to go to Beth Moore's Sunday school class and go to see her office. Well, apparently a lot of us go to the class, but few of us venture out to see the office.

I started to slip out of the conference (uh oh) to go on a little field trip. I asked the receptionist at the church where Beth's office was, and she wasn't sure. (This lady lives in Houston and has never been to Beth's office?) Well, I didn't let that deter me—I called Living Proof Ministries up and asked them for directions. They even seemed surprised. The lady who answered the phone put me on hold to see if I could come by. I thought that was odd—surely everybody goes by there. The lady returned to the phone and said that she had to be sure it was okay for me to come because people do not normally call wanting to stop by. That seemed so strange to me; nevertheless, I jotted down the directions on a sheet of paper and off I went. It was about 10:15, I was about twenty-five minutes away, and everyone at her office was leaving at noon. No problem—I had plenty of time—or so I thought.

Knowing what a mess I could end up in, one of my friends decided she should go with me. We jumped in the vehicle, took a right out of the parking lot, and headed for the Interstate. We were looking for the Highway 6 exit, and somehow we missed it. For those of you who know me, I know what you are thinking; we missed it because I was talking—but that's not what happened. The exit was not marked. There were several signs missing—including the one we were looking for! After about thirty-five minutes, we suspected that maybe we had gone a little too far, but it wasn't until we saw the sign for San Antonio several miles later that we were sure of it. It was time to turn around.

To me, this was ministering big time. In my personal life I, too, was feeling as though I might have missed an exit somewhere, and because of that I was turning around to head back. Had I truly missed an exit? Was there a sign missing that should have been pointing the way? Was I too distracted with the scenery of my life that I was not even paying attention?

As we headed back to Houston, we paid real close attention to everything—the exits, the buildings, the side streets, the mile markers—everything. Once you know you've missed something, you watch it all because you don't want to miss anything a second time. That's what I was doing in Houston. I was taking a hard look at all that had happened over the past few weeks and heading back to find the place where God had changed directions on me. That's why it was so encouraging to me when we spotted a Highway 6 sign off an upcoming exit. This sign was not clearly posted a mile or two before the exit, nor was it posted at the exit. This sign was off to the right a couple of blocks away. There was construction going on, and all the signs had been temporarily removed. There was something about it all that did not seem legal or right, but nevertheless, that's how it was. Same goes for us as we travel along God's path for our lives. Sometimes, for whatever reason, the signs have been removed and we have to search off the beaten path for direction, and I was definitely off the beaten path—I was six hundred miles from home. I realized that it's important to pay close attention to what is going on around us. The cruise control should not be on all the time. We must daily seek God's will for us. In every choice we make—big or small—we need to watch for any exits up ahead. That may mean turning the cruise control off and slowing down a little. That's what this trip had forced me to do, and I could have almost been given a ticket for traveling too slowly, but I was determined to find the turn I had missed and find my way. I was certain that if I looked closely enough I'd eventually see it.

We arrived at the offices at exactly eleven fifty-five. Talk about just making it. Our twenty-five-minute drive had taken us over an hour and a half (kinda reminds you of some Israelites, huh?). The staff was wonderful, and just seeing where Living Proof Ministries carries out its day-to-day operations was a blessing. I knew that Beth was in another city, but we were told she would be back for class on Sunday. It was well worth the drive and the time it took to get there. To me, being in Houston without going by those offices would have been like going to Memphis and never seeing Graceland (oops, I live in Memphis and have never seen Graceland—but you get the point)!

Back at the church, we realized that we had been

caught sneaking away. We were told that as far as they knew, nobody had ever skipped classes at the conference before, and they quickly determined that it was because I had never been there before! You'll be happy to know that I remained where I was supposed to be for the rest of the day, thankful for the lesson I had learned earlier while trying to find my way—to stay focused, to remain alert, and to be watchful, because sometimes the road ahead is not clearly marked. I think that could help us all!

Houston!

"For I know the plans I have for you," declares the Lord, "plans to prosper you and not to harm you, plans to give you a hope and a future."

Jeremiah 29:11

The few days I had spent in Houston had been extremely beneficial to me. I had left on a mission and felt as though I had accomplished a great deal. The time away with my girlfriends and my God had been very refreshing. It was a time of looking back and looking ahead and a time of healing and restoration, and for that I was very grateful.

Even though we were having a great time, I missed my family terribly, and I was ready to head back home. We would be leaving out the next day, but today we would be spending an afternoon in Galveston Bay. This was the final event of the annual conference that my friends had come here for. We had the best time there.

It was such a great afternoon of fellowship and fun. The people involved with First Place are phenomenal. Their zeal for God is contagious and their lifestyle very rewarding in more ways than one. It had been such a pleasure to meet them all.

It had been told to one of the ladies with First Place that I had a gift for writing and that although I had felt it, I had never seriously pursued it. This incredible lady took a few minutes out of her busy schedule in the middle of her conference to encourage me. She had written several books herself, and she gave me lots of advice. Isn't that a perfect example of how we are supposed to treat each other? Isn't that a great picture of what mentorship can look like? Sometimes it will take a few minutes of your time, sometimes it will take years, but the ripple effect can last for an eternity. Whatever your gift or talent, when you meet someone along the way who shares it, take the time to make a difference. Carole did, and I will be forever grateful.

Carole Lewis was the first person outside of my family and close friends who saw me as what I could be—as my heart longed to be—a writer. It was at that moment that I knew exactly why God had sent me to Houston. I was on a mission to meet someone who would give me the encouragement and the courage I needed to take a gift I had been given by God and not only use it, but take it seriously. My heart's desire is to write. I am passionate about it. It brings me great joy. I would leave Houston as a writer—I knew it then—God had known it all along.

I would write, and God would handle everything else …

Time to Go

Have I not commanded you? Be strong and courageous. Do not be terrified; do not be discouraged, for the Lord your God will be with you wherever you go.

Joshua 1:9

Sunday morning we were all packed up and ready to check out of the hotel. Before leaving Houston, we would attend two worship services—one at Lakewood Church and one at Houston's First Baptist, and then we would go to Beth Moore's Sunday school class.

I had asked my girlfriends if I could go to Lakewood Church. We were only about twelve minutes from their new facility. This would be the church's third service in the new Compaq Center. It is a huge, beautiful facility, and God has done great things for this body of believers. It takes three parking garages, several shuttle buses, and lots of police to handle all the people who flood the church each week. Even with all their new space, they still have two Sunday morning services! The building was massive, the music was awesome, and the preaching of God's Word was encouraging. If you ever get a chance to go to Houston, please visit Lakewood Church—even if you are not there on a Sunday, just stop by and see what a glorious thing God has done.

Next we headed to Houston's First Baptist, another magnificent church that ministers to thousands every day. Both of these churches are very community oriented. We experienced another fabulous praise and worship session, and the associate pastor delivered a life-changing message on "The Big Bad Wolf." We were having an amazing morning!

After the worship service, we headed to Beth Moore's class. Hundreds of people were there waiting on her to bring a message, and we were not disappointed. She is as passionate in her Sunday school class as she is at a conference. She has a way of communicating God's Word in a way that makes you want to know more. From the insights that she has gleaned from years of study to a fresh excitement that is evident every time she shares them, it moves you. Her teachings are changing people all over the world, and it was an honor to be in her class. She has been a mentor and teacher to me for years, and on this day, I would get to thank her in person. What a perfect finish to an amazing trip!

When we left her class, we were done—finished in Houston. It was time to go home. There was just one problem: we couldn't seem to get headed in the right direction. You would think it would be easier going than coming, but that's not always true - especially for us! I have never seen a group trying so hard to leave a state before in all my days, and as hard as we tried, we just couldn't get out of Texas! It was so funny. I still don't know what happened, but we lost our way more than once. It seemed like we had spent the entire afternoon just going in circles. (It's those crazy missing road signs in Texas!) I promise we were trying real hard to get back to Tennessee, but it just wasn't happening. It really was funny, at least to me. I kept dozing off in the back seat. Every time I woke up, we were still in Texas! Even after all this time, it still makes me laugh! I don't know how we did it, but we finally made it out of Texas and crossed over into Arkansas. We hit Tennessee sometime after midnight, and they dropped me off at my door about two in the morning. Our trip was over. I was home.

Mission accomplished in Texas. Now, what does that mean for me in Tennessee?

Hello, Good-bye

It is the Lord your God you must follow, and
Him you must revere. Keep His commands and
obey Him; serve Him and hold fast to Him.

Deuteronomy 13:4

The sun came up early that morning, and I
could hear the kids stirring as my eyes tried
to open. I said a quick prayer, grabbed my robe, and
headed for the living room where the ones that mean
the world to me were anxiously waiting for me to
get up. I had been so blessed. God had given me a
husband with a heart for him and four beautiful children. What a delight it was just to sit among them

as we talked about my trip. It was so good to be back home.

After breakfast I quickly showered and prepared to go to work. I needed to check in and just make sure everything was okay. I'd only be gone from home for a few hours. The drive to the church was one of the longest I had ever made. I had left a week ago needing to make a decision, and now I knew that time was running out. What would I do? What would I say? Nothing in me wanted to leave, but I was willing to walk away … or was I?

"If it's nothing, you're done." I still heard that over and over in my spirit, but I was still trying to change what had been done. I was still trying to come up with a way around it. All kinds of things kept going through my head as I tried one last time to get God to change his mind. "Surely, You didn't mean *done*. They really didn't mean to say *nothing*. This can't be what you meant to happen. Lord, You know that if I go I am going to be an emotional wreck. This one is going to hurt me. Couldn't You please fix it? We are running out of time here…" I wonder if I am the only one who has done this. I was begging God to stop what I knew would hurt. I was pleading with Him to do something, anything that would allow me to stay. I guess I should just go ahead and tell you that I was pitching a fit. I wish I could say that I was calm, at peace, and ready to walk into the church, gather my things, and walk out with no questions asked and no hesitation, but that is not what happened. I was determined to fight to the bitter end.

Turning into the parking lot I was still asking questions, "Are You sure You don't want me pulling in here anymore? I'm going in. Are You sure You want me to tell Pastor I have to go? Please, Lord, say something." Just then I realized what I was doing. I was asking Him to speak to me, and I realized that He had already told me what to do. I guess I should have said what I really meant was, "Please, Lord, say something else." Hmmm. This would be my moment of decision. This would be when I would take a deep breath, apologize for whining, and obediently do what I knew He had told me to do.

I remember opening the doors to the church and just taking it all in. Every moment was one that I was not sure I would ever experience again, so I walked slowly and tried to capture the way everything looked and the way everything felt because I knew change was coming. It had been coming for a few weeks. I went in to the office and sat at my desk. I glanced through a stack of mail and flipped through my messages. I could hear Pastor talking in his office. I did not know what to say or what to do. It all felt so strange. It seemed that I was back in the same situation I was in a year ago—exactly a year ago—and my heart was so sad.

I wanted my pastor to tell me that they had changed their minds; that I was needed at the church and that he did not want me to leave. I wanted him to tell me that he was sorry for all the things that were said, but he didn't. Actually, he didn't say much at all. He said hello, asked how the trip was, and went to his office. It was as if nothing had happened. It just was one more thing that confirmed what I knew I needed to do, and I hated it.

I really didn't want to do it. I didn't want to tell my pastor that I had to go. I needed a little more time—just in case. I would wait until tomorrow, but then tomorrow came, and I wondered if I'd be strong enough to say good-bye. I wondered if I would try putting it off again. It wasn't until around ten thirty that next morning that I knew no matter how I felt, I would indeed give my two weeks notice that day. It was around that time that I realized that it was August second. Dates matter to me. When dates line up, it gets my attention. Having been gone for a week, I had lost track of what day it was, not to mention what the date was. August second the previous year was the day that I began packing up the ministry office. August second sixteen years ago was the day I lost my baby. August second had quickly come to represent loss for me, and this one would be no different.

Around two o' clock that afternoon, my pastor's wife came by the office. She is one of the most generous, compassionate, and godly women I know. She often can just look at me and tell if things are okay. This day she knew that they weren't, and we stepped outside the office to talk. It took all of three seconds for the tears to start. I told her that I had to go and that nothing in me wanted to leave. I told her that I didn't think that I could tell Pastor because I was so upset. My heart was so broken. We walked into his office together and while I cried, she spoke. One more August second—one more loss.

Good-bye, Hello

Do not withhold your mercy from me, O Lord;
may your love and your truth always protect me.

Psalm 40:11

Things were weird the rest of the week as I began gathering up my things. Packing again—yuck! First the ministry office is cleared out—now it would be my church office. Why was I losing something else that meant so much to me? Why was I losing something else that I thought I'd have for years to come? Were my missions going to change every year in the army of God? If they were would I ever learn to be okay with that?

When I left the ministry office, I had wondered

if I would ever find anything that would fulfill me like it did. I wondered if I would ever be able to give 110 percent again, and if I did, would I survive the heartache it could possibly cause? The answers to all of those questions are yes. I had found a place where I felt challenged and fulfilled. I had found a place where I thought I was making a difference. I had found a place where I could give my all and then some, and now I would once again survive another broken heart.

Sunday rolled around and word had gotten out to a few people that I was leaving. Several people were looking for a job for me. One of the people who knew that I was leaving was the guy who had taken over the books back in April. You remember, he was the volunteer who was paid, but no one but a chosen few seemed to have known it. Anyway, as I walked into the sanctuary, he approached me and said, "Hey, I know why you are leaving. I lost my job Friday, so I'm going to need another one—looks like I'll be getting yours!" Let's just say that what went through my head at the moment was not very nice. I immediately turned around and went to find someone to express my concern to. My first thought was to find my pastor, but since it was Sunday morning that would not have been good, so I found a board member instead. I had spoken with him just a few minutes earlier, and he hadn't even been told yet that I was leaving. As far as I knew none of the board members had been told. As calmly as I could, I let him know that there were several reasons why I was not okay with what I had just heard, and if that guy was going to get my job, that was wrong. He assured me that was not an option, and he'd find out what was going on. With tears rolling again, I turned and walked away. Why can't I do anything without these crazy tears?

That evening I found out that the board would be meeting. Usually that means I am there; that is, unless the meeting involves me. I found out the next day that it did. My pastor called me into his office and told me that the board had decided to offer me the bookkeeper's job and $250 a week. They would pay no more than that, and I could take it or leave it. This would also mean that I would lose my position as his secretary because all they wanted me to focus on was the money. (Hindsight is twenty-twenty, but ...).

Although there was a small check (pun intended) in my spirit, I quickly decided that God had answered my prayer and come through for me in the midnight hour. Once again, I should have just run that by Him to be sure, but I didn't. I ran home to tell my family the wonderful news; only they did not think it was as wonderful as I did. Nevertheless, I was smiling again, and it sure beat the crying, so my family told me to do what I wanted to do. For me, that was easy. I'd stay. Oh, I was so happy. I got to work the next morning, threw my heels off at the front door, and went running to tell everybody that I didn't have to go. The answer wasn't "nothing" anymore, and that meant I was not done. Right?

Wrong. What followed over the next few weeks

was all my fault. Although I did accomplish what I felt needed to be done, it came at a price almost too great for me to pay.

Going...

For the Lord gives wisdom, and from His mouth
come knowledge and understanding.

Proverbs 2:6

No one was happier to be anywhere than I was
to be at my church, in my office, serving my
pastor. I was given full responsibility for keeping all
the finances in order. I reported what came in, what
went out, what we had, and a lot of times what we
didn't. There had been no budgets, no plan, no nothing for so long that the books weren't in great shape.
Within weeks, everything had been gone through,
organized, and filed. A budget was created, and plans

were being put into place. Things were great, or were they?

The previous bookkeeper was still after my job. My husband was not so happy, and my mom was certain I had made a big mistake. Mommas know a lot more than we think they do, and oftentimes when they give advice, we don't listen well, but we should. The day I had come home from work after the "ripping" I got for asking for money, my mom shared something with me. It was kind of funny because my brother came in and sat down in a chair in the living room that happened to be right between us. He didn't really notice I was crying. Mom handed me a book and asked me to read something, and I said, "If I need it, you are going to have to read it to me." Then she started crying, and my brother looked at her then looked at me so weirdly and said, "I don't know what you guys are doing, but y'all need to quit."

That's when my mother said, "No, your sister needs to quit."

See, I made the mistake of telling her about the whole, "If it's nothing, you're done" thing. And this is what she read to me out of a book she was holding: "Pray for His direction, and when He makes it known to you, don't argue with Him concerning it. Be in agreement with His will." I never should have thought any more about the situation after I knew what I should do, but I had. Not only had I thought about it, I had stayed, and my mom was very concerned about me. She did not understand how I could stay at a place and work for people who had treated me so unfairly. I could have saved myself from a lot of crying later if I would have just listened to her (and God) then.

My friends and family were not the only ones a little troubled about my decision to stay; more than once I wondered if the temper tantrum I had thrown about leaving was going to come back to bite me. At different times the words I had received from God and the words He had allowed my mother to share with me would replay over and over in my mind, and I couldn't help but think that maybe God would allow me to stay until I would not argue or complain the next time He told me to go.

Going...

When I said, "My foot is slipping," your love, O Lord, supported me.

Psalm 94:18

There was so much going on within the church and the school. There were problems that were escalating. Years of poor financial decisions were catching up with us all at once, and things would have to change. I was certain that God would see us through, and I was sure that I had been allowed to stay because God had shown me extreme favor in this position with those outside of our church. I prayed for God to show me how to best serve my pastor and my church in this area, and I asked Him for wisdom to handle all the details I faced daily. I wanted my pastor and the board to see my dedication toward the finances and my desire to see things done in a way that would bring some stability and structure to the way things were being done. I soon felt that although I did know what I was doing, the men didn't seem to care. I realized later that there was a lack of respect.

I started thinking about how I was hired in the first place, and I wondered if I had not volunteered if I would have even been given the job. There were plenty of people wanting the job, but only one who would come at no cost. Surely that was not the only reason I had been chosen—or was it? Still, I had proven to them all that I was capable of handling the responsibilities I had been given. Not only that, it was more than a job to me. Perhaps therein lies most of my problems; maybe, just maybe, that's all it should have been.

The longer I was there, the more I began to see signs of problems up ahead. Between the previous bookkeeper being very up front about wanting his old job back, the financial strains, and the lack of respect, I began wondering if it was worth it all. I wanted to do the job, but I felt as though I wasn't being heard. This became very clear in a meeting we had in the middle of September. A decision had to be made, and I knew what the options were. I presented them and it did not matter. This decision was so huge it would ultimately cost us a staff member or two. It was that evening that I began to think perhaps I was doing more harm than good. If the previous bookkeeper, or any man for that matter, would have presented the same facts, a different decision would have been made, and I was sure of that. It was painfully clear that as much as I wanted to be the one to do the job, there were limits and boundaries that some of the men would never let me cross, and the help I so desperately wanted to provide would never be accepted. Still, I held on.

Gone

The Lord is close to the brokenhearted and saves those who are crushed in spirit.

Psalm 34:18

A few more weeks went by. I kept telling myself just to give it some time. In the back of my mind I knew that there were some who were not okay with me being there, but I felt like my pastor was. For me, as long as he was happy and did not have to carry the full load of the day-to-day financial affairs, I could handle those who wanted me gone. Even after he allowed the horrible things to happen to me in August, I still felt a strong loyalty to him. Why? I'm still not sure. Was it because he was my first real pastor? Was it because under his ministry I realized that I could pursue the dreams God had given me? Was it his incredible wife? I don't know. I know that I had felt that God had allowed me to join the staff to serve him, and that's what I wanted to do, no matter what. Those are questions that I still do not have answers for today. Perhaps I will never fully understand why or how things went from so good to so bad in a year's time.

The day finally came toward the end of October that brought everything crashing down. I could no longer deny the hurt. I could no longer hold it all together. I could no longer stay. This is probably going to sound very trivial compared to the other reasons I had for leaving, but nevertheless, this one had me packed up and gone within the week.

My pastor called my husband to ask a favor. He wanted to get out from under his car lease and needed his help. This was what my husband used to do, and within an hour he had my pastor out of his Lexus sixteen months early with no penalties. Pastor asked my husband and I to go with him and his wife to turn in the vehicle. We would make a long day of it on Friday. Finally we would all be together. This had needed to happen for months, and I was so excited; that is, until the phone call on Thursday. My pastor called to ask me to get someone to get a church van ready for Friday. Why? He had invited the previous bookkeeper and his wife to tag along. I promise you at that moment I knew it was over—all of it—and it hurt a thousand times worse than it had the first time. Perhaps it had to hit me hard enough and strong enough that leaving would be my only option. It was at that moment that I wished I would have left in August.

This trip for me was crucial. Not just for me, but for me and my husband. The year had been a difficult one. We had needed our church on a personal level, and it just hadn't happened. I was sure that was what the trip was for, but now we would not be going. I was sure that the previous bookkeeper had finally convinced Pastor to let him back in, and there was not room for both of us. Maybe I should have mentioned to Pastor the significance of the trip—how important it was to me—and how certain I was that it was going to bring healing, restoration, and a better, stronger relationship between all four of us. Instead of being the thing that would draw us closer, it was the thing that ripped us all apart.

Instead of the four of us being together that Friday, I was writing the letter that would tell my pastor I had to go. I cried all weekend long. I was so hurt. I felt betrayed and used. All the emotions came rushing in. All the things that had happened over the last year—all the good and all the bad—flooded my mind. It was during this time that my husband shared with me all he had witnessed and experienced over the years at our church and how the last few months had only confirmed what he had been feeling for a long time. As he talked I listened, and I wondered how we would ever be able to remain at our church.

Sunday morning, with tears falling once again, I passed out the letters that would help me to say good-bye. Pastor did not say anything to me about the letter until Thursday when he told me not to come back in on Monday. When he left, I called my husband, and together we packed up my office. I handed my keys to a dear friend and I walked away. Broken, hurt, tired, and sad, I walked away. My family and friends were so relieved that I was finally out of that place, but for me it would take time—lots of time.

Help Me, Lord

Come quickly to help me, O Lord my Savior.
Psalm 38:22

It had been two months since the Thursday I left. The drama was interesting, to say the least. You probably would not be surprised to learn that the previous bookkeeper had taken over where I left off. He was in the office the day after I had gone. Many have said that they expected no less—still I had. I was sure everything I had done had been undone, and only time would tell if it matters if you do things right and openly and honestly.

I sent an e-mail to my pastor explaining why I felt the way I did. He replied and basically told me that he had not done one thing wrong. Maybe not, maybe so, still whether he saw them as right or wrong, they had still impacted me in a very harmful, hurtful way. No "I'm sorry." No "Hate it didn't work out." No "Thank you." No "Sit down and let's work all this out." Just the words, "Go, and have a nice life."

The board? Well, as I took my concerns to the chairman, he had nothing nice to say to me at all. Actually, he made the board member who spoke with me in August look like a saint. He laughed at me, did not want to hear anything I had to say, and then told me to let it go or leave the church. I left the church.

How do you stay when you have seen a side of your leadership that displays such brutal coldness? How do you respond to the ones you once served, once prayed with, once fellowshipped with when they turn on you? I'm sure that they feel I am entirely to blame, but I will always know the truth, and I will always know that it did not have to end the way it did. I know that for a fact. God was not glorified in any of it, and He will ultimately take care of all of it.

It was so hard to stop the tears. It was difficult fighting the feelings of bitterness and anger. I understand the power those emotions can have over you if you let them. They are like a spiritual cancer that has to be aggressively fought. Leave it unattended even for a moment and it can overtake you. There is also a part of me that is still in shock over the magnitude of yuck (for lack of a better word) I have experienced. I had heard about what could happen if you got too close, but until it happened to me, I did not believe it. It was true. It was all true.

Keep the Faith

You need to persevere so that when you have done the will of God, you will receive what He has promised.

Hebrews 10:36

So, the assignment was over. No office. No pastor. No church. I had been at a similar place before. I had felt much the same way I was feeling at that point. The same things made their way across my mind that I had thought before. Two years and two amazing but heartbreaking assignments are over. Both of them have ended the same way, and now that I think about it, they both began a lot alike too—from sheer joy to complete devastation. One minute

I am having the time of my life—the next minute I am fighting for my life. A little turmoil starts, and then *boom!* Everything's different. Both times it has felt like a bad war story. We are all in the mess hall eating and laughing, completely oblivious that there is a missile headed our way. The next thing you see is utter destruction. The missile hits and completely changes everything. The way you look, the way you feel, everything. You find yourself dazed and confused, wondering what just happened. Your clothes are torn, your friends are scattered, and the place where you were just having fun is gone. That quick. Both times. Weird, huh? I promise that's what it felt like.

I found myself once again face down, wounded on the battlefield of life. I was weak and tired, and nothing in me wanted to move. I just wanted to lie there until all the pain was gone, but in God's army that is not an option. He calls to me to come. He doesn't want me recovering on the battlefield—he wants me resting in His arms. I must've looked a mess to Him. I felt bruised and battered all over—inside and out—yet, He gently picked me up and held me while I cried. As soon as I was able, He placed me back down, and it's there that I had to decide what to do next. I could remain there, or I could accept what had happened and move on.

Because of the promises found in God's Word, I knew that with His help I could overcome anything and everything—including all of this. To overcome would require daily, intense times of renewal and refreshing. To overcome, the Scriptures would have to become my favorite food and prayer my drink of choice. It was this kind of relationship between me and my Father that would bring me through—this time and every time.

I sat and replayed the last few months all over again, trying to analyze and understand it all, and I came to the conclusion that I may never figure this one out. I did this same thing a year ago. We cannot always figure out why certain things happen the way they do, but we must trust that God does and accept the fact that He is working things out for our good. I am going to have to trust that in God's plan for me and my life this was all necessary. I know that God never wastes a moment or an experience. There is a purpose for it all. We can be certain of that because of all that we read about in the Scriptures. There is something He is trying to show us, develop within us, or remove from us. That is what mattered, and that is why I chose to move on. The pastor was not my enemy. The church was not my enemy. There is but one enemy that we fight and war against, although he always tries to disguise himself. Knowing who my one and only enemy was made my choice to move on the only option I had. If I stopped, he would win, and that's never an option for me, nor should it be for you!

I would find a purpose in my tears. I would find a purpose in my loss. I would find a purpose for this last assignment, and I would regroup. I would get up and dust off my pants, dry my eyes, shine my shoes a little, and await my new assignment. Would it break my heart? There was a good chance it might. Would it last for just one year? It was possible. So, why go? Why get up and go again? There are two reasons: the enemy hates it every time I do, and every time I do, I remind him of the loser that he is; and because my God is going with me, and I have decided that wherever He goes, I'll go. Wherever he leads, I'll follow. I love Him and will serve Him with my whole heart. Through trials and heartaches and joy and laughter, I'll go. There is a plan He has for my life. There is a purpose He has for my life. That assurance gives me hope for tomorrow. That assurance gives me strength for today.

I want God to surround you with that same kind of hope and strength as you follow Him. No matter what you are facing right now. No matter what you've already walked through. No matter what tomorrow holds—never give up, never quit, never surrender, because God is working out every necessary detail of your life. Sometimes it hurts, sometimes it doesn't, but ultimately it all works out for our good.

What's next for me? I don't know—but God does—and that brings me peace. I have peace because I completely, totally, uninhibitedly trust Him. I trust Him to quiet my broken heart. I trust Him to place me where He needs me. I trust Him to show me the way. I trust Him to remain with me always. I trust Him so I keep going. Even when it hurts, I keep going. When my flesh is screaming, "It's just too hard," or, "It's just not worth it!" I keep going.

We have to. We have to keep going. We have to keep fighting. We have to keep pressing on. Through loss, through heartache, through good times and bad, press on. He loves you, and He'll see you through it all. Trust Him.

Keep the faith!

A Promise

Every word of God is flawless; He is a shield to those who take refuge in Him.

Proverbs 30:5

Difficult journeys will change your heart. Mine did. Sometimes our hearts change for the better; sometimes they don't. Choices have to be made in the dark times. I have experienced unexpected loss and almost unbearable tragedy over the years. Most people believe that it takes this kind of pain to really rattle your faith. During these intense times of pain, our faith can be shaken to the core, and you either grab hold of God and refuse to let go, or you turn and walk away. If you trust God and seek Him with all that you have, you will experience Him in ways some never have, and you'll know Him in ways that some of us could not even comprehend. To those of you who have endured, I thank you. Your faith is an encouragement to me and to those around you. You see, we may not all experience the same degree of pain, but we'll all experience it on some level. We will all have to decide what we will do when difficult, hard times come our way. Whether it's a rebellious teen, an unsaved husband, or the loss of a loved one, life can and does hurt at times. But God is so faithful. His promises are true and they are solid. His Word will be concrete under your feet when everything else disappears. His Word will be the sweet song in your heart when you can't even hear the music, and His Word will be an anchor to secure you in the storms.

To make it you must know Him—I mean really know Him. You must know His Word. You must pray and read your Bible. You must study the Scriptures. Of all the steps and advice I could give to those of you scarred by life's unexpected changes, nothing would be as important as knowing God by knowing your Bible. It doesn't even matter if you were hurt twenty years ago or ten minutes ago; the Word heals. I promise, if you'll grab hold of the living, relevant, life-sustaining power of God's Word, you will make it. Open up His Word. Make a commitment today that you'll read something every day for at least five minutes and go from there. Don't make it hard. I have found that the Psalms are appropriate anytime, anywhere you are. Start there. Ask God to help you understand and watch how His Word will heal you and sustain you.

You will make it. I made it. Even though many times I was kicking and screaming, I made it. Even when my life was being rearranged and my future repositioned, I made it. I made it because I knew God. I didn't just know about Him; I knew Him. That's what reading His Word every day will do for you. I knew from Scripture that others had walked bumpy roads and survived. I knew that God was always, all the time, with me. I knew that because I had made reading His Word a priority in my life. Open it up, take it in. I promise you that His promises never fail, and they are more than enough to see you through.

Hallelujah, God is good!

A Prayer

"Though the mountains be shaken and the hills
be removed, yet my unfailing love for you will not
be shaken nor my covenant of peace be removed,"
says the Lord, who has compassion on you.

Isaiah 54:10

It is my prayer that you will always keep your toes
close to the heels of our Father through the good
times and the bad. That you will hold onto His hand
as He leads you through the twists and the turns of
this life. And most of all, that you will be sheltered
under His loving, tender wings when the winds of
change begin to blow.

Draw near.

Hold tight.

Stay covered.

God bless you on your journey.

Part Two

Where can I go from your Spirit? Where can I flee from your presence? If I go up to the heavens, you are there; if I make my bed in the depths, you are there. If I rise on the wings of the dawn, if I settle on the far side of the sea, even there your hand will guide me, you right hand will hold me fast.

Psalm 139:7–10

Introduction

As Part Two begins, it has been almost two years since the winds of change began to blow. The storm that nearly took me out ultimately failed. Was it easy to overcome? No. Was it as simple as just moving on? Not hardly. It was a difficult and painful process; one that God had to lead me through because left on my own I would have never made it. He alone is due all the praise and glory for my restoration and my healing. It was His strength, His love, and His compassion that saw me through, and I will be forever grateful. As God settled the storm around me and the winds died down, I found that the changes God made in my life were all for my good.

These changes, although good for me, were very difficult. Going through them, it felt as though I was in the middle of a ravenous hurricane with pieces of me and my life being violently tossed around. One by one the pieces had to be picked up and examined and then released—released to a God that could handle them because it was too much for me. My faith had been tested, my joy had been stripped, and my peace had been stolen, but as the rain began to stop and the sun began to peak though the clouds, I realized that I had made it. I had made it because God had been faithful. He had seen me through the storm just like He said He would, and I was going to be okay. I found myself surrounded with a sense of calm that I hadn't felt in years, and I was ready to put all the things that had happened behind me. It had been intense. It had been painful. It had been devastating. And I was about to find out that it had also been just the beginning…

The Storm is Over

He calms the storm.

Psalm 107:29

I can still remember the day I realized that the storm was over. It was early on a Thursday morning, September 14. It was my birthday, and I was sitting at my desk answering the phones at City Auto Sales in Memphis. I reached over and tore the top sheet off my desk calendar that revealed the day's scripture. It was 1 Samuel 12:16, "Now therefore, stand and see this great thing which the Lord will do before your eyes." As I read that verse, I felt an unmistakable peace in my spirit and an undeniable love in my heart, and I will never forget it.

I had become so accustomed to the wind and the rain that I hadn't even realized that the winds had died down or that the rain had begun to stop. I suppose there was a part of me that didn't think the storm would ever cease. It had been nearly eighteen months since I saw the first few sprinkles, and it had been a non-stop downpour ever since.

Many of those stormy days were very hard for me, and at times my emotions were all over the place. I'd be singing in the rain one minute, and then I'd be crying face down in the mud the next. I was one diagnosis away from bipolar disorder and one fit away from Lithium. Have you been there? For whatever reason, the loss of my church had me questioning everything. I questioned my faith, my beliefs, my observations, my thoughts, my intentions, the things I did right, the things that I didn't, and everything in between. If I had not known God in such a personal way, I would've turned away and run from Him. I had done it before, but that had been a long time ago. Now I knew enough about Him to trust Him, and I did—I just didn't understand Him. He had removed me from a church I loved, from a pastor that I gladly served, and from a church family that meant so much to me. I know we are not supposed to question God, but I did. For months I begged God to tell me why he had allowed this to happen. I finally reached a place (probably out of exhaustion) where I quit asking. I just held onto the answers I did have. I held onto His promises.

I knew that God was looking out for me. I knew

that He could see way beyond my present circumstances. And I knew that He had everything under control … even if I didn't! Before the storm had even started, God knew exactly what I would go through, exactly what I would struggle with, and exactly how He'd show me that the storm was over. He would use a scripture on a desk calendar, and He would also make sure that at that very moment, I would know that He was closer than I ever dreamed He could be! Do you know that I still have that calendar page? It's pinned up on my bulletin board in my office, and it serves as a constant reminder of that day and of His faithfulness to me.

His faithfulness to me (and to you) is strong and steady and good for us, whether we are on the mountaintop or in the valley. Our circumstances change, but He doesn't. Our faith in Him wavers, but His faith in us never does. He is Faithful and True … always has been, always will be. He calmed the storm that was raging in my life, and He will do the same for you. Never give up on Him. He will cover you in the rain and protect you from the winds until the storm is over.

The Dream Giver

The Lord will fulfill his purpose for me; your love, O Lord, endures forever—do not abandon the works of your hands.

Psalm 138:8

One of the best things about the storm being over was the peace I felt. Not only was the storm calm, I was calm. I remember spending the first few days just in awe of what He had done. I felt good. My life felt good. Everything was good. That was huge for me. There was a time within the storm that I was certain that I would never feel okay again. I thought that even if God did deliver me, there would be no way I would ever fully recover from what had happened. I was so wrong. The moment that God calmed the storm surrounding me, He also calmed the storm within me. I was amazed—completely amazed—and my God was just getting started.

Over the next twelve months, I saw God do some great things, just like He told me He was going to do. He did great things in me and with me, and He touched every area of my life. I felt like Cinderella. You know her story—she's had a hard time, nothing is going her way, and she's trying to do the right things, but it doesn't seem to matter. Then the fairy god-mother shows up and changes everything. Cinder-ella watches in amazement as everything she needs is given to her. You see it too: the horses, the carriage, the dress, and those shoes! Everything she needed— there—one right after the other, and because of that her life was changed forever. That's what the next year felt like for me. Everything I needed—there— one right after the other, and because of that my life was changed forever!

The biggest thing that happened to me during this time was seeing my journal that I had kept dur-ing the storm become a real, self-published, paper-back book. Usually what I write is only for me to see, but this time I decided that I would write for my children. I know they wondered if I was going to be okay, and I needed them to know that I would be. I was hoping that these journal pages would do that. I also hoped that they'd see how important a personal relationship with God is. For most of my life, I didn't understand how personal my relationship with God could be or was supposed to be. I wanted my kids to know. I also wanted them to know that even when life doesn't seem all that good, God is!

When I had finished writing, I printed out the pages and put them in a three-ring binder, but I wanted it to be special. I did a little research and found a printing company that would allow me to take my journal pages and create a paperback book. Two weeks after I emailed the files, I received a paperback copy of the words I had written. Shortly after that, through circumstances that only God could have arranged, my book was on the shelves at Davis-Kidd Booksellers in Memphis. That led to my first book signing and my first TV interview. I loved every minute of it! That book, *The Winds of Change,* is part one of this book now, but back then it was a book by itself. Holding that small paperback book, I realized that if God could fulfill one of the dreams that He had placed inside me, then He could fulfill them all, and once again I found myself in awe of Him.

What Was That?

Be sober, be vigilant; because your adversary the devil walks around like a roaring lion, seeking whom he may devour.

1 Peter 5:8

I was having the most amazing, life-changing, incredible year ever! I began to realize that God was shifting things in my life to make sure I didn't miss what I was supposed to be doing. I believe that during this time, God was aligning my passions with my purpose, and when the two of them collided, so many things in my life started making sense. I now knew that writing had something to do with my calling—with my purpose—but I also knew that there was more to it.

I began searching for what was missing. I asked God to show me the big picture, and then I begged Him to show me the next step to take, and He did. I was at Davis-Kidd's, and a book caught my eye. I took it off the shelf and flipped through it. I then scanned the entire section, pulling off several other books. I placed them all on a bench and sat down beside them to look through them. I flipped through all of the books that I had stacked up beside me, and I left that day with the first one I had seen.

When I started reading the book, one of the first things I noticed was that the authors had a website, so I pulled it up. I was thrilled when I saw that they offered classes, so I went to find one close to me. There wasn't one. What happened over the next nine weeks could take me hours to tell you—so, to save time—here are the Cliff Notes. Ready?

There was a note at the bottom of the webpage that said, "If there is not a class near you, click here to find out how to bring one to your area," so I clicked it. I filled out a form and hit submit, I was sent an application, went through a series of interviews, was offered the opportunity to conduct the classes, had to find a ton of money, found it, flew to Cleveland, got trained, got my certification, came home, rented an office, scheduled my first class, and then went back on TV. Whew! Fun, huh?

It was fun! Everything about this year had been fun. My book was selling, my job was great, my finances were better, and I was three days away from starting my new business. All of this made me think about the scripture in Romans—the one where God says that He will take everything the enemy meant for evil and make it good. The enemy had meant for the storm to take me out. He had meant for it to make me bitter and angry and ineffective, but it hadn't worked. It hadn't worked because God had held onto me. It hadn't worked because God used a simple journal I wrote for my kids during the storm to change everything. Had I given up, those pages that were written may have been long gone by now, but I didn't, and they aren't. The very thing that the enemy meant to destroy me had backfired, and now it was being used against him. The enemy had hit me hard, but my God had just hit him back!

I felt invincible, but as I started doing one of those celebration dances like they do in the NFL after they score, I heard a noise off in the distance behind me. It wasn't rain. It wasn't thunder. It was more of a cracking sound, and I immediately sensed that something wasn't right. I stopped dancing and turned around. I remember thinking, *Surely not. Surely the enemy's not that stupid. Surely there's no way he would come after me again.* I hesitated for a moment, wondering if I should run and hide or turn around and keep dancing. I took a deep breath in, exhaled slowly, then turned around and started moving my feet! *So what if he's out there,* I thought. *So is my God...*

Wait a Minute

"For my thoughts are not your thoughts, nor are your ways my ways," says the Lord.

Numbers 6:26

"Momma, come quick, Granny needs you!" Those were the words my son yelled as he came running through the front door, and those were the words that I will never forget. The look in my little boy's eyes told me that something was wrong with my daddy. I ran out the front door behind him and ran to my parents' house next door. When I opened the back door, I saw my mom and dad standing in the living room. Daddy was holding onto his walker, and my mom was trying to hold him up. When my eyes met hers, I knew. My daddy was having another stroke.

I helped her get Daddy to the bathroom and then out on the porch. He was still talking to me, but his speech was very slurred, and the whole left side of his face was drooping. I had seen him like this before. Usually this required a short stay in the hospital. He was calm; I was calm. Momma was a wreck! I sat with Daddy and tried to help him drink his coffee while Momma got dressed and packed their bags. Within a few short minutes, I could tell Daddy was getting worse. I grabbed a cold washrag and wiped his forehead. He could still talk to me as we were putting him in the truck. Daddy didn't like ambulances, so we put him in the truck. Momma drove and I followed. We were headed to the hospital . . . again.

As I was driving, I began to cry and I began to pray. I adore my Daddy. I am and always will be a daddy's girl. He and I were very close, and I hated to see him sick. He had already survived a severe heart attack, three strokes, and an abdominal aneurysm, and I just didn't know how much more he could take.

When we arrived at the hospital, they assessed Daddy fairly quickly and confirmed that he had a stroke. Daddy was still able to talk to us, but he was very sleepy. We had been at the hospital maybe an hour when we realized that this stroke was different. It was one o' clock, and a neurologist had come in with some flashcards and asked Daddy to tell him what he saw. Daddy couldn't do it. Daddy's speech was now almost unrecognizable, and I was barely

able to tell Momma what he was saying. By two o'
clock, Daddy had fallen asleep. Momma and I were
certain that he'd be better when he woke up, so she
and I sat by his bed waiting ...

Daddy slept and slept. Even when they trans-
ferred him to a room upstairs at seven that night,
he slept. I left the hospital around eight and told
Momma that I would be back in the morning. I had
barely been home ten minutes when the phone rang.
It was Momma and she was crying. Daddy had quit
breathing. They were able to resuscitate him. My
daddy was now in the ICU in critical condition on a
breathing machine, and he was in a coma.

The next morning we were told that Daddy's
chances of waking up were not good, and that if he
did wake up, he'd never be okay again. I went in and
stood beside his bed. I thought about my birthday
just two days before and how perfect everything
had been, and then I thought about that noise I had
heard. The cracking that could have only meant one
thing—there is trouble up ahead.

I took my daddy's hand and I began to pray. I
asked God to tell me if He was about to take my
daddy home. I had done it before, and I had always
been given a peace that Daddy was going to be okay.
Thankfully, this time was no different. God assured
me that my daddy would wake up ...

Are You Serious?

When my spirit was overwhelmed within me, then you knew my path.

Psalm 142:3

I t was Sunday again. Seven days had passed since Daddy had slipped into a coma, and the diagnosis for him was getting worse every day. The week had been a hard one. We had been faced with so many difficult decisions. On Tuesday, the doctors put in a temporary feeding tube, and on Wednesday, they told us that they wanted to do a tracheotomy on Daddy so they could take him off the machine. We knew Daddy wouldn't want that. So we asked them if they could ease him off the machine and let him try and breathe on his own first. They did, and he did, and it was good. The next day, the doctors wanted to put in a permanent feeding tube. We knew that Daddy didn't want that either. We were told that the feeding tube wasn't a permanent thing and that it could be removed if and when he didn't need it anymore. The problem was that we didn't want to put him through anything like that unnecessarily. We were torn as to what to do. We just kept asking the doctors for a little more time and asking God to help us make the right decisions.

As each day got harder and harder, I held onto the promise I had received from God—the assurance that Daddy was going to wake up—and I told everybody that would listen. Sometimes people didn't want to hear it. I was told that I was in denial. I was told that I needed to quit saying that and just accept the fact that Daddy wasn't ever going to wake up. I was told to accept the fact that my daddy was already gone, but he wasn't and I didn't; well, except for about an hour…

I had walked over to my momma's house. She had come home to sleep, wash clothes, and repack. She had been crying, and I asked her what was wrong. We sat down on the couch, and she told me that before she left the hospital, she signed the "Do Not Resuscitate" papers. I stayed a little while longer and then walked back home. I could feel so many emotions inside me, and for the first time since Daddy had fallen asleep, I was about to lose it.

I walked in the front door and sat down on the

couch. My husband was watching football and playing cards on his computer. He didn't say anything to me—didn't ask me about Daddy—he just sat there. I finally told him what was going on, and I began to cry. I looked at him and I told him that I wasn't okay and that I needed him to hold me for a little while. He just looked at me and then started playing cards again. For a minute, I really wasn't sure what was going on. I couldn't believe that he'd just sit there with me so upset … but he did.

I stood up, walked to my daughter's room, fell across her bed, and just wept. I was crying so hard that my other two daughters heard me from their rooms at the other end of the house. My girls laid down beside me, and we all cried together. I cried until there were no tears left. I heard my husband get up and walk to the kitchen. I heard him get some water. I watched the doorway, wondering what I would say when he came into her room, but he didn't come. The next thing I heard was our bedroom door shut. I couldn't even begin to understand what had just happened. How could my husband of eighteen years do that to me? How could he not be there for me? Why didn't he hold me, and why didn't he seem to care about me at all? I was so hurt and so confused and so angry. That night was the first night I would cry myself to sleep because of my marriage. Sadly, there were a lot more ahead.

Faith, Don't Fail Me Now

Watch, stand fast in the faith, be brave, be strong.

1 Corinthians 16:13

Monday, September 25, Momma was headed back to the hospital, and I was on my way to work. I felt like I was in shock. I was still trying to figure out why my husband didn't hold me. I was angry because I shouldn't have had to ask him in the first place. Our marriage had been through a lot over the last few years, but we had made it. I knew things were different between us because of all that had happened, but what I hadn't realized until the night before was that things were so different that I didn't even recognize my husband anymore. The man I married would have held me. The man I married would have been there for me way before I had to ask.

We had married in 1989. We had four children, three daughters, and a son, ranging in ages from ten to seventeen. Our marriage had been a good one, and we were going along just fine until a series of events over a four-year period left us both a little different than we were before. These things had hurt me, him, and our kids, but I didn't realize at the time how deeply my husband had been affected, and I wouldn't find out until much later. All I knew at this time was that he was not happy. He was very quiet. We only talked about the things that were necessary—never anything below the surface. He would get up, go to work, come home, go to sleep, and do the same thing the next day. He didn't seem to enjoy anything anymore. I believe that he focused on the things that he had lost instead of focusing on the things he had left—like me and his children. I didn't understand. I didn't know what to do. I was tired of trying to reach him. I had been thinking that I was the reason he was so unhappy, and after what had just happened the night before, I was sure of it.

Later that day, I told my husband that it was time we got some help. I wanted us to get counseling, but he refused to go. He said we'd be fine. It wasn't what I wanted to hear. I began thinking about my daddy still in ICU, still in a coma. It had been eight days. I thought about how life had been a little over a week ago. Everything seemed to be so perfect, but now there appeared to be another storm brewing. Maybe that was thunder I had heard a few days ago …

I left work that evening, and while I was driving to the hospital, I began to talk to God about what I was thinking and feeling. I was going over the events that I had written about in my first book, and I was thinking about how much worse all this was already. I had described those events as feeling as though I was in the middle of a hurricane and I thought, *If that was a hurricane, what is this?* At that moment, God dropped the words *when the levee breaks* into my spirit, and I immediately thought about Hurricane Katrina. Hurricane Katrina hit the Gulf Coast with intense rain, wind, and had caused a tremendous amount of damage, but the hurricane itself was only the beginning.

The storm had passed, and the people in the affected areas thought that the worst was over and that they had made it. But then, just as everyone began to breathe a sigh of relief, the levees around the city of New Orleans gave way. The hurricane had brought the rain that had strained the levees, but it wasn't the storm that actually caused the complete and total devastation to this city. The city had survived the storm, but everything changed when the levees broke.

When the levees broke, the city was destroyed. As I sat there in the parking lot of the hospital, I put my head on the steering wheel and just cried. The sound I had heard—the cracking sound—had been the levee around me. I knew that the water was coming, and I begged God to hold onto me.

Defying the Odds

For great is your love, reaching to the heavens;
your faithfulness reaches to the skies.

Psalm 57:10

Tuesday, September 26, my daddy and my marriage were both in critical condition. It's a life or death struggle for both of them. It was so hard to comprehend exactly what was happening. I kept thinking that just days ago, my daddy and my marriage had been okay, and now they were both struggling to survive. I was so glad that I had the day off. I got the kids off to school and lay back down. I was so emotionally drained. I had so many things going through my mind, and I was trying to keep everything in perspective. I was trying to stay focused on my faith. I was trying to stay calm. I knew that God was close, and I knew that as long as He was, I would be okay no matter how high the water got.

I waited on the kids to get home from school before I left to go to the hospital. My oldest daughter, Ashley, was going with me that day. We got to the hospital around four forty and went to find Momma in the critical care waiting room. We hadn't been there but a couple of minutes when the receptionist paged the King family to take a call. Ashley and I walked with Momma over to the phones. I will never forget what I heard on my end. "This is Carolyn … what … he is … right now … okay." Momma hung up the phone and said, "Your daddy's awake and he's asking for us. They want us up there right now."

He was awake? He was asking for us? The doctors had told us that even if he did wake up, he probably wouldn't know us or ever be fully alert, but if he was asking for us, they were wrong! We hurried up to the ICU waiting room. We walked over to the nurse's station and then we saw him. He was awake! Praise God! My daddy was awake!

He looked out into the hall, and his eyes met Momma's, and we ran into his room. He was trying to say something. He had to repeat it a few times, but I finally figured out what he was saying.

"I got sleep," he said.

I looked at him and said, "You got sleep?" and he said, "Yeah." That's my daddy—so adorable—so amazing—and now, after being in a coma for eight days, so awake! I kissed him on the cheek and then looked up toward the heavens and thanked my God for waking my daddy up!

I was so happy that Ashley had come with me. It was great watching my daughter, his first grandbaby, sit there beside him. Daddy loved all of his grandchildren so much. He was such a family man and so proud of all of us. My momma and Ashley stayed beside Daddy as I began calling everyone. It was so incredible to be able to tell our family and friends that Daddy was awake. I couldn't tell them much else, but for right now that was all they needed to hear. They would move Daddy from the ICU that night, and the next day there would be a steady flow of family and friends coming to see him. I was so thankful, so very thankful!

With God, Daddy had once again defied the odds. He was awake, alert, aware of where he was and what had happened, and even his memory was intact. We would soon find out, though, that Daddy had been seriously affected by the stroke. His journey from this day forward would be a difficult one but one that he would take one day at a time with his God close beside him.

Excuse Me?

Trust in him at all times, O people; pour out your hearts to Him, for God is our refuge.

Psalm 62:8

My daddy was out of immediate danger, but his condition was still very critical. It was now the second week in October. Between work and the hospital, I hadn't been home much. I was there now, though, and would be all weekend. I had missed my babies, and there were things I needed to get done around the house. Toward the end of the day, I was just about finished and sat down to take a break. I thought it would be a good time to go through the mail.

I had sorted through all the junk mail and was going through the rest of it when I saw an envelope that had been returned. I didn't recognize the name on the front, but I knew it was my husband's hand-writing. I will never forget what I saw when I opened that envelope. It was a letter my husband had written to his first wife from thirty years ago! It said, "… I have thought of you every day for thirty years … I didn't mean it when I said that I didn't love you … I made a covenant to God to love you forever, and I will…" I didn't even know what to think. My husband, the one I had asked to hold me and hadn't, the one I had needed, who couldn't be there for me, could sit down just five days later and write to her?

Excuse me? This woman who has haunted our marriage—the woman he was married to for six months the year I was in kindergarten—the woman who hadn't bothered to find him, talk to him, or reconnect with him since the day she left—this woman is the one he loves? Are you kidding me? I was so far past upset. I was so far past angry. In our eighteen years of marriage, I had never felt like this. The way I felt the night he wouldn't hold me couldn't even compare to how I felt at that moment. Before I had felt hurt; now I felt betrayed, and I felt like our whole marriage had meant nothing to him. I was so mad. He came in the back door that night, and for the first time since we had married, I yelled at him. I was crying when I handed him the letter.

"Why did you open that?" he said. "Your name is

not anywhere on that letter. It has nothing to do with you. It's none of your business."

Excuse me? What? I said that it had everything to do with me, and I was yelling and crying, and he told me to go take some PMS pills and leave him alone.

I was just shocked—and furious. How could he do that and then talk to me like that? Did he honestly think it was none of my business? I knew that he had some regrets with his first marriage, and a few years back I even tried to find her because I knew there were some things that he wanted to tell her. Who does that? Who tries to help her husband make peace with his former wife? I don't think there would be many. And now, when I needed him the most, all he was concerned about was her?

After he came in the living room, I told him that if he had needed to write that letter, he shouldn't have done it behind my back. I also told him that the letter was my business and that it had really hurt me. He said that he had just wanted to finally get some peace, some kind of closure. He also said that it was over; he had done what he felt he needed to do. He didn't want her, and he wasn't ever going to look for her again. I was still too shocked to really say or do anything else.

Did my husband really believe that what he had done was okay? Did he really believe that it was none of my business? Yes, he did. He lied to me that night. It wasn't over, and he had every intention to look for her again.

Classmates.com

The eternal God is your refuge, and underneath
are the everlasting arms.

Deuteronomy 33:27

Fast forward to February 2008, I am in counseling for the first time in my life. I had finally
gotten to a place where I knew I needed some help.
Things had calmed down, but I was having trouble
trying to get over the two things that had happened
within my marriage. Even though things had been
okay on the surface the past few months, I was still
deeply hurt by the abandonment and betrayal I had
felt. I knew that even if my husband would not go
with me to counseling, I had to. I felt like it was my

responsibility to do all that I knew to do to save my marriage, and nothing else seemed to be working.

I was a bit surprised at the things that I learned about myself and my marriage during those first few sessions. As bad as I wanted my counselor to tell me how to fix my husband, she was only interested in fixing me. She helped me work through the emotions I was having, and she showed me how to step back and look at the big picture and not just the area that I seemed to always be focused on. By the middle of April, I thought that things were getting much better.

For the first time in months, I was at a place where I thought that maybe I might be able to move past what he had done to me and that our marriage might not really be over. I had been with this man for eighteen years. We had married after knowing each other just six weeks, and we had what most believed to be the picture-perfect family. My husband was an ordained minister. He had a doctorate in theology. He had also been through hell and back over the last few years, and the enemy had been relentless. The enemy wanted nothing more than to see his world come crashing down. I saw that, but he didn't. This time the enemy was after our marriage. I had fought for our marriage for years. I had prayed for my husband, and I had begged God to protect our kids. When I married him, I vowed to stay with him no matter what, and that's what I was doing. I was convinced that God would not let the enemy destroy our marriage.

It wasn't until I logged into our joint banking

account and noticed that my husband had paid thirty-nine dollars to join classmates.com that I thought maybe I was wrong. I knew what this meant. I knew that he was looking for his first wife again, but how could I prove it? I didn't want to ask him, and I didn't have a paid classmates.com registration to look him up. That Friday night, my husband was out of town, and I sat down to use his computer. Now, I know that none of you would have done this, but I did. I pulled up his e-mails and found the ones from classmates.com that linked me right into his profile. There I saw the message he had posted on his high school chat room page, and I was right. He was looking for her.

This time, I didn't want to confront him right away. I knew that he'd talk his way out of things again. He had made his mom think I was crazy for getting so upset about the letter that came back in the mail. He even made me feel like I had blown everything way out of proportion, but I knew there was more to it, and this time I needed to know exactly what was going on, so I had to be careful. I needed the truth from him, but I knew he would never just tell me. I had to figure out a way to get the information I wanted. I wanted to know what he was thinking, what he was doing, and what that meant for me and my marriage. I desperately wanted the truth, and I was willing to do anything to get it.

Ninety-Nine E-mails

Then you will know the truth, and the truth will
set you free.

John 8:32

Looking back, perhaps I should have just asked
him about the classmates.com thing, but I
didn't. I really didn't think he'd have done anything but
get defensive. The funny thing is that if he would have
just told me that he wanted to join classmates.com to
look for his first wife, I probably would have set up his
account. It wasn't the fact that he felt like he needed to
find her that was the problem; it never had been. The
problem was that he was trying to do it behind my back
and that he felt like it was none of my business. Maybe

if he would have handled the letter episode better, I wouldn't have done what I did next.

I decided to set up a fake e-mail account so that I could contact him through classmates.com. I became Sara, and I sent him two e-mails—one where I told him I had known his first wife and that I might be able to help him find her, and a second that asked him three questions: Why are you looking for her? Where are you living? Are you married? About an hour later, I received a response from my husband that stunned me. Not only had he answered her e-mail, but he had told her things in this e-mail that I had never known. All I wanted was enough to confront him with the truth, but I had gotten so much, so fast, I decided I wanted more.

Over the next six days, we would send each other ninety-nine e-mails—forty-three on Wednesday alone! At one point that day, I was on the phone with him as me and responding to his e-mail as Sara. This man, who barely had thirty minutes a day for me, now had hours to e-mail Sara. He liked her. Honestly, he liked her a lot. I remember thinking that Wednesday evening that he didn't like Sara—he liked me—I was the one he was talking to. I was the one he was flirting with. I was the one he was opening up to. I was completely swept up in it. I really never meant for it to go on like it did, but just when I would tell myself that I wouldn't respond to him again—I would find out something else that would have me wanting to know more.

I suppose the thing that I learned that hurt me

the most was how he truly felt about me and her. He nicknamed his first wife Soulmate, and he nicknamed me Safe. She was the one he felt was his true love, and I was the one that was in the right place at the right time. Another thing that hurt me was when I found out the truth about the ring he had worn on his right hand since the day I had met him. He had told me that it was his granddaddy's ring and it was very special to him. He told Sara something completely different. This ring was a ring that his first wife had given him. He told Sara that it meant so much to him because it was all he had left of her that he could feel and touch. This meant that for eighteen years, he had her ring on his right hand and our wedding band on his left. I found out a lot more than I should have, but I did get the truth, and that's what I was after.

I had gone to Miami that week, and on Saturday night in a hotel thousands of miles from home, I got an email from him that finally just ripped my heart out and I snapped. I told him that it was me and not Sara on the other end that he was e-mailing. I told him why I had been Sara, why I had asked him the things I had, and why I felt like I had to be her to get the truth. I had been lied to for months and I didn't know what else to do. Perhaps this wasn't the best way to get to the truth, but it had worked and at least now I knew, but this left him furious. I asked him what we were going to do and how we were going to get past him lying to me again. When he popped back up in my inbox, I saw, "Kiss my ___!"

A Marriage ... Broken

The Lord upholds all those who fall and lifts up
all who are bowed down.

Psalm 145:14

I arrived back at the airport on Monday afternoon. My brother had come to pick me up, and
I could tell that something wasn't right. He told me
that Daddy had another stroke and that there was
nothing that could be done for him. The affects of
this one were mild and slowly faded away, but it
reminded us again just how fragile Daddy was. We
pulled into the driveway, and I went to see my daddy.
I had been gone for five days, and I had missed him.
He had missed me too.

I didn't stay there long. I told them I would be back in the morning. I needed to see my kids, and I wanted to be there when my husband came home from work. We had e-mailed each other on Sunday and tried to make some sense out of what had happened. We didn't talk much about the e-mails, just about what was going on between us. I was in the bedroom when he got home. We opened a bottle of wine and just held each other. I don't think either of us said anything. Inside me somewhere, I knew that he was not in love with me anymore, but I also believed it was because of the pain that he had let build up in his life over time. I believed that I was brought into his life to save him from himself. I don't think that either one of us had felt in love with the other for some time, but we did love and care about each other. I have never been one to focus on the bad side of things, but I do believe at this point I was in complete denial of what was really happening. I believed that if I held on and stood by my husband that God would work out the knots that we had both tied in our marriage and straighten everything back out again.

We went to sleep that night and woke up the next day and everything was okay. I went to see my counselor that afternoon and put the thirty-two pages of e-mails on her desk. I told her what I had done, but that I was okay because I finally knew the truth, and that's all I had wanted. The first thing she said to me was that I was crazier than she thought. She said that she'd never had a client ever do anything like I had done. She started reading through some of the e-mails, and she asked me about some of them. She was concerned because I wasn't upset, wasn't angry—I really wasn't anything. She told me that she thought I was in shock. She said that there was no way I could have processed what I had found out and not feel anything. She said that my mind couldn't handle the stress of my daddy's condition and the damage that the e-mails had caused. My counselor also told me that there was no way that my husband was okay with what had happened and that he really didn't have to be. She said she had no doubt that he was beyond furious with me. I told her she was wrong. She asked me to talk to him about the e-mails and see what his reaction was and then to call her.

A couple of nights later, I made sure that all the kids were gone, and I waited for him to get home so we could talk. After he changed and came back in the living room, he made a few comments about the house and about me, and everything was good. Everything was good until I asked him about the e-mails. He said, "What e-mails?" I said, "The ones from last week." He then went on to tell me that he had sent those e-mails to Sara, not me, and that he'd never talk about them because they weren't meant for me. When I pushed it, he got dressed and walked out. There would be two more incidences over the weekend that were a direct result of the e-mails, and neither of the incidents was good. My counselor was right. He was beyond furious, and I was in shock.

I Love You, Daddy

God will redeem my life from the grave; He will
surely take me to Himself.

Psalm 49:15

With my marriage still a mess, my parents
place had become my second home. My
daddy was at home recovering. He was still paralyzed
on his left side, making it impossible for him to do
anything on his own. If you would have known my
daddy, you would have known that the only thing he
never wanted to happen to him was for him to get
to a place where he couldn't take care of himself. He
never wanted to have to be waited on and cared for
like he was now. I knew this would be a problem for

him. When he first came out of his coma, I told him how close he had come to dying, and that if God would have been ready for him, he wouldn't still be here with us. I told my daddy that there was still something that God needed him to do here.

A few months after that conversation around the end of November, my brother and his wife found out that they were expecting their first baby. When I told Daddy the news, the first thing he said was that must be why God woke him up and left him here. He said that if God could wake him up, then God could let him stay until the summer. It was now July, and the baby was due any day. Daddy was still here and he was doing really well, considering everything that was wrong. I mean, we had been told that he wasn't going to wake up in September, that he wouldn't make it until Christmas, that there was a good chance he wouldn't make it until his birthday in April. Still, here we were in the middle of July, and Daddy was still here with us.

Connor Wallace King was born on Friday, July 11. I was at the hospital when the baby was born. He was so precious. I left there to go and let Momma come to the hospital, and Daddy and I talked about baby Connor. Daddy couldn't wait to see him. Daddy hadn't left the house in months, because traveling was hard on him. The next day, my brother and his wife and his new baby left the hospital to bring Connor to meet his paw-paw. Daddy was so excited. He was up in his wheelchair and sitting at the front door when Brad pulled in the driveway. Brad got out and opened the back door to get his son. He walked through the front door, got his baby out of his seat, and brought him over to Daddy. I had never seen someone so glad to see a baby before ever. Daddy had held on just to see this baby. Daddy was certain that this was the thing that God woke him up for—the thing that God had needed him to do.

Daddy spent those first few days with baby Connor propped up beside him. He would rub his little leg with his good hand and just talk to him. It was the most beautiful thing I had ever seen. My daddy was so proud. He was proud of all his grandbabies, but this one was his namesake, his son's son. We took pictures and got some videos, cherishing the moments Daddy was getting to spend with Connor.

On that Tuesday, just four days after Connor was born, Daddy's leg began to swell. A nurse was called in, and she said that she believed that there was a blood clot somewhere and that we needed to get him to the hospital right away. The ambulance was called, and we were on our way. The hospital confirmed that there was a blood clot and Daddy would spend the next several days there. When I went to see him that Monday, Daddy told me that it was almost time to go. It was the first time he had said that to me, and I knew that he was right. Daddy asked his doctor to let him go home the next day. After seven days in the hospital, Daddy returned home. The next Tuesday, July 29, Daddy passed away with his family, including little baby Connor, in the room with him. I loved my daddy so very much.

Till Death Do Us Part

The Lord is good, a refuge in times of trouble. He cares for those who trust in Him.

Nahum 1:7

Daddy's visitation was so sweet, and his funeral was so beautiful. Daddy touched so many lives, and we had so many people come out to pay their respects. While people were coming in to say good-bye, we were getting to introduce little baby Connor to everyone. Daddy had said one time that he was going and Connor was coming, and that was how it was supposed to be. He said that's just how life works. We knew that Daddy had fought hard to stay until Connor got here, and we knew he was able to leave this world with no regrets. He was a happy man, and he wanted us to be happy.

My daddy loved my husband, and he was proud of him and all that he had done for me and the kids. Daddy knew that my marriage was in trouble before he left. He knew that I had gone to talk to an attorney. I wasn't happy. My husband wasn't happy. The kids weren't happy. I had gone to discuss my options after things continued to get worse between us. One night when I was at my parents' house, Daddy noticed that I was crying. He also knew why I was crying. He had always encouraged me to stay with my husband as long as he worked and took care of me, but he knew that I was needing more. His baby girl needed to be loved. He looked over at me the night I was crying, and he tossed me his towel that he kept near him. He looked at me and told me to do whatever I needed to do, that he was proud of me, and he just wanted all of us to be okay. I knew that was him telling me that if I decided that divorce was the only way I felt like things could be okay, that I had his blessing.

One week after he had passed away, I got an e-mail from my husband telling me that he thought it would be best if we separated for a while. He told me that he didn't want to bring it up while Daddy was still here. He wanted to know if I would go and stay at my mom's for a while. At first, I was so mad. I felt like he had been wanting to do that for a long time. I wondered how he could ask me something like that in an e-mail. I sat there and thought about all that had happened between us. I thought about the way I had needed him this past year. I thought about the ways we had let each other down and the ways we had hurt each other. My counselor had suggested that we try separating months ago, and I just didn't push it. I had been staying at my momma's most of the time anyway over the past few months, so maybe this wasn't a bad thing. I opened the message, clicked reply, and sent him the message that told him I would stay at Momma's.

At Momma's, there was peace. Inside our house next door, there wasn't. I needed things to be still and quiet for a little while. I needed time to deal with my daddy's death and to deal with my broken marriage. I needed time to think, and I needed time to pull myself together and try and figure out what I wanted and what I didn't. The only thing I did know was that I did not want to be divorced—the other thing I knew was that I didn't want to be married either.

My marriage was supposed to last till death do us part. The enemy had hated the calling on my husband's life, and he also hated our marriage. He relentlessly went after everything that was sacred to us. Still, sleeping on a couch at my momma's, I believed that God would only let the enemy do so much before He made him back away. There would be a great testimony to share on the other side of the mess we were in if we didn't give up—if I didn't give up—and at least for now, I was still holding on.

Save Nola

For the Lord your God will bless you in all your harvest and in the work of your hands, and your joy will be complete.

Deuteronomy 16:15

It was now October, and I was still at my momma's. Even though we were separated, my husband and I talked every day. I would even make dinner and leave it for him some nights, and I would make a pot of coffee at some point during the day so that he'd have it the next morning. I was back and forth between my house and my momma's house a lot. The girls stayed at one house most of the time, and my son and I stayed at the other. It was a weird separation, and it was a weird situation. It was also one that was starting to get old. I was very tired, and I was still very lonely.

I did try to stay busy, and I was most of the time. I had started a new job working full-time, and I had also enrolled in college to get my degree in psychology. I was finishing my second book and still working my own business, Your Passionate Life. It's this business that encompasses everything I am passionate about, and it allows me opportunities to not only reach women locally but across the country, and I was about to make a trip for an event that was being sponsored by the National Association of Women in Construction (NAWIC) Chapter 339. I'd first met them when I spoke at a Regional Convention for NAWIC in Tunica, Mississippi, the previous April. I love the NAWIC organization, and I love these women from NAWIC Chapter 339. They are amazing, strong, passionate women, and I was thrilled when they asked me to come.

It was about ten days before I was scheduled to leave. I had arranged to fly and go alone, but this all changed when a couple of my very best friends decided that we should make a road trip out of it. I had only known these ladies about a year, but they had become such an important part of my life that I couldn't imagine how I had made it this far without them. This road trip was something that we had needed for a long time, and I knew one other person who just had to go with us: my daughter Kasey. We would leave on a Sunday morning headed to Louisiana. I knew that God had rearranged some things so that I was here with them and not on a plane by myself. The event itself was more than I had ever hoped to experience, but now I would also get to experience the fun and the excitement that you can only find when you pile up in a vehicle and head out on a road trip!

On my trip to Houston, I had written about ten things I had learned as I traveled with some of my other friends. On this trip, I would learn some more. Before we get back to our story, I'd like to make a little detour and share with you ten things I learned as we traveled to and from Louisiana. Here they are:

1. Friends make everything more fun.

2. A GPS system becomes horribly addictive after the first use.

3. Everybody needs a rest area every now and then.

4. A familiar scent can transport you to a happy place instantly (trust me).

5. When yo momma is callin', you betta answer da phone.

6. Expect unexpected stops along the way.

7. Starbucks coffee cup bottoms can just fall out and get you really, really wet.

8. Sometimes detours are necessary and take you places you never meant to go.

9. NOLA isn't a big fish.

10. Every day is like a road trip, so pay attention, buckle up, and enjoy the ride!

Just like last time, each of these things taught me a little bit more about myself and this world that we live in. I could spend hours writing about them, but for now, I'm only going to share one. I suppose out of all of them, this is the one I am asked to talk about more than all the rest. It's where the title for this chapter comes from and where we all enjoy the most laughs. There wasn't much that was funny about this last year for me, but this definitely was. Here is the story about how I found out that NOLA isn't a big fish.

It was Monday morning, and we were headed to Bourbon Street. Having never been to New Orleans, I was looking forward to seeing the area that I'd only heard about. When we got to Bourbon Street, we could see the gulf, and Melanie pointed to an area where there used to be a big aquarium. She said that it had been destroyed during Hurricane Katrina, and it didn't look like it had been reopened. I didn't think much about it until I kept noticing something on T-shirts and bumper stickers and even on some of the windows. I kept seeing things like "Love NOLA" and "Save NOLA," and I promise you, I didn't know what that meant. I finally decided, being the intelligent person I am, that it must have been a big fish or something that they had in the aquarium (kinda like the save the whales thing), but I couldn't understand why there was no picture of NOLA on anything. I thought that was a little strange since it was apparent that they loved her and wanted to help her.

At lunch, I meant to ask my friends who NOLA was, but I forgot. Then, as we were pulling out to leave, it hit me. Don't know why or how, but I suddenly realized that NOLA meant New Orleans, Louisiana, and I felt so stupid. I really thought NOLA was a big fish that the city had lost and couldn't find after the aquarium was destroyed. Isn't that crazy? I swear sometimes I wonder how I've made it this far. NOLA … a big fish? Oh, man! It just goes to show you that God truly can use anyone!

That night I shared that story with the ladies at the event. I don't know what they thought about me at that point, but it must have been okay because they showed back up the next morning for our next session!

That story is one that I will never forget. My girlfriends will still tell me good-bye sometimes and say, "Save NOLA!" It always makes me smile. I even received a card from Nancy Lee—the incredible woman who was responsible for making sure I got to New Orleans—and on the front of the card, she wrote, "Save NOLA! J the fish!" I love it. I have it up on my office wall as a reminder of the trip, the event, and the fun I had while I was there.

I had no idea what was waiting on me as I returned back home to Tennessee. I knew that there were some decisions I would need to make soon, but in my wildest dreams I never imagined they would be so hard to make and so hard on me. I have often wondered why God positioned this trip to take place when He did. The only thing I can come up with is that I had to have realized one of my biggest dreams right before one of my biggest heartaches. Exactly one week after telling the Save NOLA story, I ended up at a place I never thought I'd be and found myself in need of some saving myself...

Save Tammy

He has sent Me to heal the brokenhearted.

Isaiah 61:1

On Monday, October 13, I had been in New Orleans having the time of my life. I was speaking for a group of women that had changed my life in a short amount of time in ways that they will never understand. It was one of the best days of my entire life. How sad that this very next Monday would be one of the worst days of my life.

I was at work when I got involved in an argument between my brother and my husband. My brother had been having a very hard time since my daddy had passed away. He was sad, then happy, good, then not so good, and on this particular day, he was very upset with my husband for something over which he didn't really have any reason to be. The problem wasn't that, though; the problem was my brother was screaming for help, and my husband just started screaming. It had been non-stop all day, and neither one of them was listening to me, and they were both really mad.

After work, I had plans to meet a friend for a women's ministry function at her church. As I was driving over there, it seemed apparent that my brother and my husband were going to kill each other. My daddy would have been so upset to see the two of them acting this way, and I just needed him to come back for a minute and make them behave. When I got to the church, I was worn out. This would be the first event like this that I had attended since Daddy passed away. The hymns and the praying and the atmosphere that should have brought me peace just made me miss my daddy more.

When I left there that night, it was close to ten p.m. I had barely gotten across town before I began having a panic attack. I had been having them regularly for about a month, and this one was really bad. I couldn't catch my breath, I was cold and hot at the same time, and it felt like someone was squeezing my heart. As I got closer to the hospital, I was trying to decide whether to stop. I finally decided that I should. By this time, I had quit crying and was able to call my momma and tell her what was going on and that she didn't need to worry about me. I just

didn't feel good, and I needed some help. I called
my husband and told him the same thing, and then I
walked into the ER.

I walked up to the desk and told the receptionist that I needed to see a doctor, and I started filling
out my name. She then asked me if I was hurting
anywhere, and all I could think was that I hurt every-
where, and I completely lost it. It took about three
minutes for them to get me in the back and start
hooking me up to everything. I had the heart machine
wired to me, the blood pressure cuff strapped on, an
oxygen mask over my nose, and an IV in my arm. I
couldn't catch my breath. I couldn't quit crying. I felt
like I was completely falling apart. It was the scariest
feeling in the world.

It took about an hour for all my vital signs and
my breathing to return to normal. They moved me to
a room, and I waited to see the doctor. He told me
that I'd had a severe panic attack. Along with that, I
was also dehydrated, exhausted, and on the brink of
a complete nervous breakdown. He asked me if I had
anything happen in my life that would be causing
me extra stress, and I started crying again. He pulled
up a chair, wiped my eyes, and just sat there beside
me until I calmed down. I told him about losing my
daddy and about my marriage. He ran some more
tests, took blood samples, and then told me that he
was going to admit me for three days so I could get
some rest. I told him that wasn't necessary. I told him
that I knew what I had to do and that I would be
okay. He agreed to let me go and sent me home with

a bottle of nerve pills, water, and some very specific instructions. He couldn't save me; God couldn't even save me this time because He had told me what to do. I had to save myself.

No Fairytale Ending

For I know the plans I have for you ...
                                        Jeremiah 29:11

I got to my momma's at four o'clock in the morning. I lay down on the blue couch that had been my bed for the last several months and tried to go to sleep. I wasn't really sure it would make a lot of difference to sleep or not because I would be getting up in an hour and a half. I did eventually drift off and woke up ten minutes before the alarm went off. It was five ten. My arm was all bruised from where they had taken the blood, and I had a horrible headache. I already had some of the medicine the doctor had prescribed for me, so I got up, took two ibuprofens and a nerve pill, and then walked over to my house to pour my husband a cup of coffee and get ready to go to work.

I saw my husband briefly that morning. He came into the kitchen while I was making my son's lunch. He walked up behind me and put his arms around me, and all I could do was cry. I couldn't help but think about how many times I had needed him to do that and he hadn't. Now, it was the last thing I wanted. I had been trying so hard not to think about how bad I needed to be held, and I was so angry at him for letting me get to that place. I knew he had his own set of problems, but I was his wife. I needed him, and he had let me down.

I had promised myself the year before on September 23rd, the night I had first really needed my husband to hold me and he hadn't, that if I was still married a year from then and I wasn't completely happy, I would file for divorce. I wasn't happy, I hadn't filed for divorce, and I was dying inside.

In the ER, I had spent a lot of time praying and a lot of time thinking about everything that had happened. I needed help and I needed to know what to do. I knew that my husband and I were not in love with each other. I knew that things had gotten really bad. I also knew that most couples go through things a lot worse than we had and they had made it. I began to lay there and pout. I did not want to be divorced. I did not want my family to be ripped apart. I didn't. I just didn't. The very last thing I thought I would ever have to face was divorce. For me, the only way that we could avoid it was to seek help. I needed to know that my husband wanted me and that he wanted to save our marriage.

A few days later, I told my husband that I wanted to come home and that we were at a place where I felt counseling was our only option because of all we had both been through. He told me that counseling was not an option, and he offered no other solution. I said that we could either go to counseling and stay married or that we could go to court and get a divorce. His response? "When do you want me out of the house?" At that moment, I knew my marriage was over.

Assessing the Damage

I am with you and will watch over you wherever
you go, and I will bring you back to land ...

Genesis 28:15

Ifiled for divorce six days later. We really didn't
have the money to hire lawyers, so I Googled
my way through the divorce. I filled out all the
papers, gathered all the information we needed, and
gave them to him that Sunday afternoon after I had
signed them. He took the papers, looked through
them, signed them, and handed them back to me.
There were no tears, no "I'm sorrys," no yelling ... no
nothing, but that was how it had been for a long
time. My husband and I could be friends. But we

couldn't be married. By this time, we were both just done.

You may be wondering how an ordained minister can let go of his marriage. You may also be wondering why his wife may have ever felt like she could quit trying. I can tell you that the only way I can explain how our marriage and our family were destroyed was because the enemy is very real. He taunted us for a long time. He had messed with my husband for so long that he no longer wanted to live—not even for me or for our kids. He was so angry, so withdrawn, so sick, so unhappy, and he was killing me. I had done all I knew to do.

Counseling wasn't an option and neither was church. Our last trip inside of a church together was the day after I had gotten the letter back that he had written to his first wife. I had walked into the church that day, and for the first time ever, I didn't smile and portray the perfect family image that people were used to seeing. I was still so angry, and I didn't care what anybody thought. After that, he never went back to church with me. We weren't even praying together anymore. I had prayed for us without him up until the classmates.com thing. After that, I stopped going to church, and I also quit praying. Once you get to that point, you are in serious trouble, especially when you know better. Where we had ended up would call for some serious intervention. In the end, I felt like counseling was our only option, and he felt like it wasn't an option at all.

Our kids were not surprised by our decision.

They had been watching everything that was going on. They knew that we weren't happy and that things weren't right between us. It broke my heart to know that we weren't enough to make my husband, their daddy, want to get better. Why would someone choose to remain depressed and withdrawn and miserable when there was so much at stake? Even if he didn't want me anymore, why wouldn't his children be enough for him to want to get help? I don't know the answer to that question, and I'm not even sure my husband did either.

As I am writing this, it has been a year since I filed for divorce. My husband of nineteen years is now my ex-husband, and he is now engaged to someone else. We have had some dramatic moments in the last few months, but it seems that things are finally starting to settle down. I don't understand why a lot of the things that have happened were necessary, but once again I trust that all of it served some sort of purpose, even if I never know what that purpose was this side of heaven.

There are days when I think about what happened to our family and it makes me sad; other days it makes me mad, and other days it doesn't bother me at all. I go to sleep every night knowing that I did everything I could do at the time to make things work. When we got to the point where I could do no more and he refused to do anything, our marriage ended.

Are You in Good Hands?

The Lord is good to those whose hope is in Him,
to the one who seeks Him.

Lamentations 3:25

S o the damage had been done. The water from the levees surrounding me had hit its peak, and it was now starting to recede. Once again I was looking around at a mess. I could hardly believe that I was still standing. There was a part of me that was lost during the flood, but there was also a part of me that was found. There was a marriage destroyed but two lives that were saved. There was a daddy now absent from this earth, but one who is alive and well in heaven. There were children who had learned to tread the waters but are back on dry land now. There were dreams that had washed away, but there were new ones left behind.

I see ... my broken home filled with the broken hearts of my children. They are hurting, but by God's grace, they are going to make it. They are some of the strongest people I have ever met, and sometimes I just can't believe that they are mine. They are still, and always will be, the most cherished gifts I have ever received. I hope that when they look back on all that has happened, they will know that I never meant for them to ever get hurt. I also hope they know that just because bad things happen, it doesn't make God mean or unfair or untrustworthy. I hope that they know that the only reason their momma knows that everything will be okay is because she is still holding onto God, and He is still holding onto her.

I also see ... my new bedroom that is at the other end of my house. I had to leave my master bedroom for a while. I moved and fixed myself a bedroom where I could rest, where I could heal, and where I could begin again. I was able to work some overtime at the end of the year, and I even had a new bed and dresser. I am surrounded by my books and my pictures, and I love it. I even have my favorite red chair in there. In this room, I have spent some peaceful nights in a bed that is mine alone. My new bedroom has become a sanctuary for me. There is peace in this room and actually, for the first time in a long time, there is peace in this house.

I have lived in this home for most of my life.

I moved in here with my parents when I was just seven years old. Since that time, I have spent only about two and a half years living somewhere else. This home was given to me shortly after I married. I brought all of my babies home from the hospital through its front doors, and each of my children have, at one time or another, had the bedroom that was mine when I was growing up as their own. This is my house and theirs, and it is our home.

I stop to think about all that has happened and realize that I have once again been protected from something meant to destroy me and rescued from something meant to break me. Do you know why I made it … again? How I survived when the levees around me broke? It was because I was in good hands. Alone I would have surely perished, but my God made sure that I would come away from this better than I was before. The trauma, the losses, the pain, the hurt, the grieving—all of it—left me weak, lonely, tired, broken, and at one point in the ER in the middle of the night, but God had seen me through it all. I had made it, and I was ready to rebuild my life because … my God protected me … again … my God rescued me … again … my God set my feet upon dry land … again … and my God was faithful to me … again.

There is only one way to overcome the things that this life is destined to deliver to your doorstep, and that's by being in good hands … in God's hands. He's the best coverage you'll find when the enemy decides to show up. Tell me, "Are you in good hands?"

A Promise

For no matter how many promises God has made,
they are "Yes" in Christ.

2 Corinthians 1:20

God's hands have amazing power and strength. They will never fail you or harm you or let you go. For those of you who are holding on to Him, your name is even written on His hands. Picture that for a moment with me ... my name (and billions) of others, are there, written on God's hands. Can you even begin to imagine how big those hands must be? I can tell you that they are big enough to protect you from anything and everything the enemy brings your way. That is a promise you can hold on to. Good days or bad, God's promise to protect you never fails.

As I was picturing God's hands and thinking about how much love He has for us to do the things He does, I thought about His heart. They say your heart is about the size of your fist. Think about those hands again; think about the size fist God's hands must make and the size of His heart. No wonder He can love us all the way that He does. No wonder He's there right beside us all the time. We are all so loved. That is amazing to me, but what's even more amazing is that even those of you who haven't even acknowledged His presence in your life, who've never accepted His love, who've never even bent your knees to make Him your God, are still so adored by Him. You are so loved by Him that He sent His Son to save you from an eternity in hell. Many of you may feel like your whole life has been hell, but can I tell you nothing anyone has ever been through on this earth comes anywhere close to what Jesus suffered on the cross or the hell that awaits unforgiven sinners forever.

I saw a sign the other day that said, "Life Has Many Choices. Eternity Has Two. What's yours?" and it's the truth. It's also true that by not making a decision, you've made one. You are the only one who can accept or reject the promises of God. My daddy was a good man, but he lived without God for most of his life. I prayed so hard for him. I begged God to save him. God did all He could do, but nothing changed until my daddy accepted God and made Him the Lord of his life, and that brings up another very important point. Words alone don't impress God. We've all seen those people who say a prayer on Sunday (or Tuesday—you can be saved on any day ending in a y) but are acting a fool on Monday. Maybe you could use the saying "Talk is cheap" here. God not only wants you to talk to Him; He also wants you to live for Him. Without a change of heart, a change of attitude, it's not enough.

I'm not saying that you have to be a saint every day. It's not about keeping up with your church attendance, time spent on your knees, or even how many times you lose your temper. It is about making a commitment to build and maintain a genuine, personal relationship with God—one that will not only see its ups and downs but get you through them too. A relationship with God is the most important thing, and it is the only thing you will take with you when it's your time to die. What would God say if you showed up before Him today? When you see Him face to face, what do you want Him to say to you? It all depends on you, and the decision that you and you alone choose to make.

I made the decision a long time ago to accept the promises of God and make Him the Lord of my life. I love Him, follow Him, and obey Him as best as I can. I have failed Him many times, but still He keeps me close. I have fussed, pouted, screamed, and even asked Him to leave me alone. I have also prayed, loved, obeyed, and asked Him to forgive me, and He has. Through it all, His promises have remained true. Accept Him. Trust Him. Love him.

A Prayer

You will keep in perfect peace him whose mind is steadfast, because he trusts in you. Trust in the Lord forever, for the Lord, the Lord, is the rock eternal.

Isaiah 26:3–4

It is my prayer that when you face your darkest hour, you will turn toward the light, you will reach for the One who is right there beside you, and you will find strength in Him when you are weak.

There is nothing about this journey we are on that takes Him by surprise, or that makes Him second guess His ways, or that removes the love He has for us. He is the One that makes a way when there is no path left in front of us. He is the One that moves the mountains when there is no strength left to climb. He is the One that meets the floods when there is no way to escape and the current is pulling us under.

I don't know where you are today, but what I do know is that you are not where you are by accident. Nothing that happens in your life is an accident. Whether good or bad, it is part of the journey pre-destined for you. If you will allow God to lead you, to protect you, to love you, and at times perhaps carry you, you will make it through it all. Never give up. Never quit moving. Never lose hope. You can trust Him completely. In Him, you have all you'll ever need and then some. I have witnessed that in my own life over and over again.

As I type the last few words, I am thinking about you and praying for you. I may not know you, but I know that God does. I may not know what you are going through, but I know that God does. He's the reason I am here, and He's the reason you are here.

It is my prayer that somewhere in this story, you have found something that you can hold on to and that you have gotten a glimpse of the One holding on to you …

He loves you and so do I.